S0-DMH-860

Keto Diet Cookbook for Women after 50

The Ultimate Guide Book Ketogenic Diet Lifestyle for Seniors. Simple Keto Recipes and a 21-Day Meal Plan - Balance Hormones, Regain Your Metabolism, Shed Excess Pounds, Burn Fat, Lose Weight Fast, and Stay Healthy.

By **Nigel Methews**

Contents

INTRODUCTION

An active metabolism is the key to good health! The rate of metabolism does not remain the same, however! As a person ages, the body naturally goes into a slow metabolic cycle. This process of aging speeds up when we consume unhealthy food and live an inactive lifestyle, resulting in a range of metabolic disorders and other related diseases. A dietary approach and a healthy lifestyle are, therefore, an essential need for all the people who want to avoid early aging. Health issues are widely common among women over the age of 50, as they suffer from natural bodily changes due to menopause. Osteoporosis, arthritis, high blood pressure, obesity, and inflammation is common among women of this age. These conditions can, however, be prevented by consuming a ketogenic diet and following the scientific lifestyle of intermittent fasting. In this cookbook, we shall extensively discuss the perks of both the diet and the fasting approach in relation to their effects for women over 50 years of age. A set of 90 ketogenic recipes and a meal plan is there to provide you with a well-written guideline to start your keto-fast regime.

CHAPTER 1: Why Keto?

The ketogenic diet emerged as a successful dietary approach back in the 1920s. It was put through several experiments and tests until the diet became popular among the general public. From movie celebrities to athletes, everyone promotes the ketogenic concept as a secret behind their fitness. The discovery of this low carb and high-fat diet was a groundbreaking one, as it revealed a healthy role of fats in a diet when consumed without much of the carbohydrates. The ketogenic diet was at first used to treat the patients of Alzheimer's and epilepsy, but then the diet showed remarkable results in preventing and controlling other health disorders like:

1. Diabetes
2. Insulin resistance
3. Cancer
4. Cardiac diseases
5. Obesity
6. High blood cholesterol
7. Acne
8. Aging

The ketogenic diet provides a natural means to stimulate the body's metabolism, which then prevents the risk of such disorders. This diet initiates ketosis, a natural body mechanism that is the real reason behind the success of the ketogenic diet.

Is the Ketogenic Diet Healthy?

The National Center for Biotechnology Information has published multiple studies stating the claimed benefits of the ketogenic diet through clinical evidence. The diet was tested on both men and women to find out its pros and cons, and the tests revealed that it significantly reduces the tendency of weight gain and helps lose weight. In women, especially, the diet was tested to identify the impacts, and it showed marked effects over the metabolism. With certain exceptions, the ketogenic diet—when consumed with the complete understanding and knowledge of the diet—proves to be healthy.

High Fat and Low Carbohydrates Explained

The ketogenic diet works through ketosis. This natural metabolic process can only occur when a person reduces his carb intake. Therefore, the diet restricts the use of all the high-carb ingredients. Carbohydrates are those macronutrients that are readily and quickly broken down into simple sugar, and quickly spikes up the blood glucose levels. Consistently increased blood glucose levels can cause insulin resistance, diabetes. Since carbs are easily digested, when a person consumes any food containing both the carbs and fats, the carbs are broken down to meet the energy needs, and the rest of the fats are stored in the body leading to high cholesterol and heart diseases. But when the proportion of carbohydrates is reduced compared to the fats in the diet, the body resorts to fats to meet the energy needs, and they are broken down to release energy and ketones through the process of ketosis.

Therefore, the ketogenic diet prescribes the use of fat-rich substances like all vegetable oils, nut oils, cheese, cream cheese, butter, and creams. On the other hand, it restricts the daily carb intake to only 50 grams or less. On a ketogenic diet, a person must avoid the intake of grains, legumes, starchy vegetables, high-sugar fruits, sugars, sugary beverages and drinks, and all other products containing these basic items. These ingredients must be replaced with non-starchy vegetables, sugar-free products, meat, seafood, and nut-based milk and processed dairy items.

Getting into Ketosis

The process of ketosis is named after the byproduct, which is produced along with energy when a fat molecule is broken down. It is known as a ketone. When a person switches to the ketogenic approach, his body too switches to ketosis to meet the energy needs. It metabolizes fats and produces more ketones than usual. These ketones are mainly responsible for decreasing the oxidative stress of the body and detoxify the mind and body. Thus, ketosis works in three ways: by reducing the carb intake, it controls weight gain; then it provides energy through the breakdown of fats, which is more lasting; and finally, through the release of ketones, it regulates improved metabolism.

Signs That You Are in Ketosis

Since the human body heavily depends on carbs, it always takes time for the body to adapt according to the new ketogenic lifestyle. It's like changing the fuel of a machine when the body is switched to the ketogenic diet; it shows some different signs than usual, which are as follows:

1. Increased Urination

Ketones are normally known as a diuretic, which means that they help in the removal of the extra water out of the body through increased urination. So high levels of ketones mean more urination than normal. Due to ketosis, more acetoacetate is released about three times faster than the usual, which is excreted along with urine, and its release then causes more urination.

2. Dry Mouth

It is obvious that more urination means the loss of high amounts of water, which causes dehydration as more water is released out of the body due to ketosis. Along with those fluids, many metabolites and electrolytes are also excreted out of the body. Therefore, it is always recommended to increase the water consumption on a ketogenic diet, along with a good intake of electrolytes, to maintain the water levels of the body. It helps to incorporate more salty things (like pickles) into the meal.

3. Bad Breath

A ketone, which is known as acetone, is released through our breath. This ketone has a distinct smell, and it takes some time to go away. Due to ketosis, a high number of acetones are released through the breath, which causes bad breath. It can be reduced with the help of a fresh mouth.

4. Reduced Appetite and Lasting Energy

It is the clearest sign of ketosis. Since fat molecules are high-energy macronutrients, each molecule is broken down to produce three times more energy than a carb molecule. Therefore, a person feels more energized round the clock.

CHAPTER 2: What Does the Ketogenic Diet Mean to Women After 50?

Body Changes after 50

A living being keeps evolving throughout its life. Every age brings a new set of changes. Similarly, being over 50 always leads to significant changes in the body, which mainly includes:

1. Lowering of the collagen production, an important protein that helps in the rejuvenation of skin, hair, and nail cells. Thus, reduced collagen production leads to wrinkled skin and poor hair growth.

2. Dry skin: When the skin loses its elasticity and collagen, it gets drier and rougher in appearance.

3. The weakening of bones is another symptom of this age, as the bones no longer absorb calcium, and cartilage also suffers deterioration. It is particularly common among women, usually resulting in osteoporosis and arthritis.

4. Menopause: In women, menopause marks a significant change in the body. The reproductive system ceases to produce eggs, and the menstrual cycle stops for good. These changes occur under the influence of hormones and also lead to hormonal imbalances.

5. Weight gain: Reduced rate of metabolism in this age leads to obesity and weight gain. The calories that are consumed are not actively consumed but rather stored in the body in one form or another to cause obesity.

6. Enlarged heart: High blood pressure and weakening of the muscle cells gradually leads to the enlargement of the heart. This may, in turn, cause more cardiac complications.

7. Decreased memory recall: The degeneration of brain cells is another effect of aging, and it leads to memory loss.

Benefits of the Keto Diet for People over 50

The above-discussed effects of aging can be reduced or controlled to some extent using the ketogenic diet. When the entire ketogenic lifestyle is followed along with dietary changes, it results in the following known benefits:

1. Accelerates Metabolism

As a person ages, it is the rate of metabolism that slows down with time. Metabolism is the sum total of all the processes that are carried out in the body. The building of new cells and elements, as well as the breaking of the existing agents into other elements. The fat-sourced high energy and release of ketones accelerates the rate of metabolism in the body.

2. Hormones Production

It is said that a woman's body is particularly more sensitive to dietary changes than the male body. It is mainly because there are several hormones that are at play in a woman's body. With a slight change in dietary habits and lifestyle, women can harness more benefits out of their fasting regime. Hormones in women's bodies are not only responsible for regulating the mood and internal body processes, but they also affect other systems in the body. Controlled release of energy and a healthy diet is responsible for maintaining the balance of estrogen and progesterone in the body.

3. PCOS

Polycystic ovarian syndrome is another common disorder that is prevalent among women of all ages, especially those over 50. PCOS cases are often the result of the consistently high levels of insulin in the blood. Therefore, the ketogenic diet, due to its lowering of insulin effect, can treat or prevent PCOS to some extent. It can also control and counter the negative effects of PCOS in women.

4. Diabetes

Insulin resistance is a condition in which the body resists producing insulin. When the body fails to produce insulin, the pancreatic cells produce more insulin to lower the blood glucose levels. The excessive insulin production over a longer period of time ultimately wears out the pancreatic cells, and they lose the ability to produce necessary insulin levels, thus leading to diabetes. Since intermittent fasting can prevent insulin resistance by naturally lowering the blood glucose levels, it also reduces the risks of diabetes. The ketogenic diet controls the insulin levels in the blood, thus prevents the risks of insulin resistance and diabetes.

5. Oxidative Stress

There are various chemical reactions that are occurring within the human body as a result of metabolism. These reactions produce millions of products and byproducts. Some chemical reactions produce free radicals which are highly reactive in nature. When these radicals are left in the body for a longer duration of time, they can oxidize other elements in the cells and mingle with the natural cell cycle, ultimately leading to cell death. The cumulative effect of those free radicals is termed as oxidative stress. When this stress increases, it can negatively affect human health. Ketones produced through ketosis work as antioxidants, which removes the free radicals and toxins from the body.

6. Cures Cancer

The ketogenic diet also improves the immune system, which helps patients to fight against all sorts of diseases, especially cancer. When the body undergoes ketosis, there is an increased production of lymphocytes that kills the pathogens, or agents, that may lead to cancer. Several cancer treatments also use this natural immune system to fight against the cancerous cells.

7. Inflammation

Inflammation is the swelling of body tissues and organs for any practical reason. In women over the age of 50, inflammation can result from the hormonal or electrolyte imbalance. Accumulation of uric acid and high sugar and cholesterol levels may also cause inflammation. Diseases like osteoporosis, or arthritis, which are common among women, also cause inflammation. Similarly, inflammation can also occur in the brain due to Alzheimer's or dementia. In any case, inflammation is always painful and health-damaging. Ketosis can help the body fight against the agents, causing inflammation. It promotes the immune system to increase its productivity. The damaged cells, which cause inflammation in the neighboring area, are then actively removed through autophagy to clean the body and repair it.

8. Weight Loss

Finally, weight loss is the most promising and obvious advantage of the ketogenic diet. Women over 50 years of age actively seek the keto diet to lose weight. It can reduce two to three pounds of weight within a week.

Ketogenic Diet and Menopause

Menopause always results in great stress for every woman, as there are several physical and psychological changes a woman goes through. The effects of menopause vary for each woman; it all depends on age, genetic makeup, living conditions, and diet. Menopause is characterized by the following known effects:

> - Insulin resistance
> - Poor Sleep
> - Weight gain
> - Brain fog
> - Dry skin and hair
> - Stress reactive
> - Hot flashes
> - Mood swings
> - Increased risk for heart disease

The weight gain alone can lead to further complications and severing of other symptoms like insulin resistance, lack of sleep, hot flashes, etc. During menopause, the fluctuation of the two hormones, estrogen and progesterone, makes the body more stress reactive and insulin resistant. The disadvantage of being insulin resistant is that there will always be high blood glucose levels, which will lead to diabetes. All such effects of menopause can be prevented by switching to the ketogenic diet.

Most Common Mistakes and How to Fix Them

Every beginner is prone to commit some mistakes since the ketogenic diet is not a simple diet. It requires vigilant and careful meal planning and an understanding of the diet. Here are common mistakes that people usually commit while following the ketogenic lifestyle.

1. Not Looking for the Hidden Carbs

Where people mostly look for and avoid the most obvious forms of carbs as in sugars, grains, and beans, they fail to look out for hidden carbs that are largely present in processed food and market-packed products. Many food products that even say they are sugar-free may also contain a high amount of carbohydrates. By not avoiding such ingredients, people fail to achieve the results of ketosis. Therefore, practice the habit of reading the labels of all the food products and do not just rely on product tags.

2. Ignoring Nutritional Needs

Most women opt for a ketogenic diet only to lose weight. In this struggle of weight loss, they may turn a blind eye towards their nutritional needs. Controlling the carb intake does not mean depriving the body of what it needs to function properly. Therefore, meeting nutritional needs is imperative in this regard. Consume all the macro and micronutrients in your diet. Fibers, vitamins, minerals, and phytonutrients are as important as the proteins and fats for optimal brain and body function. The meal should contain a good amount of fats and protein to meet the needs of the body in the absence of carbohydrates.

3. Poor Hydration

When the body is in the state of ketosis, it loses water through increased urination. Dehydration can lead to electrolyte imbalance in the body. Therefore, it is very important to constantly hydrate yourself. The dieter must constantly drink water or other low-carb juices and smoothies to keep the body hydrated.

4. Avoiding Workouts

Most people over the age of 50 consider themselves too old to exercise as they feel weak in the bones and experience the lowering of metabolism. But exercise is proven crucial in harnessing the benefits of a ketogenic diet. A light and simple exercise routine are important to prepare the body for ketosis and the changes that come along with it.

5. No Monitoring of the Changes

Without keeping track of the changes that your body experiences after opting for the ketogenic diet, one can't really maintain this healthy routine. Most people complain that they have not experienced any change after the ketogenic diet, which is mainly because of the fact that they lose track of the new dietary routine they planned to follow. With constant monitoring, a person can also keep a check on his health conditions. Any signs of discomfort and negative effects should also be looked for.

CHAPTER 3:
Intermittent Fasting and Keto Diet

What is Intermittent Fasting?

Fasting is basically defined as a deliberate abstention from eating. It is the deliberate action of depriving the body of food and calories for more than six hours. Intermittent fasting is one of the forms of fasting in which the fast is carried out in a cyclic manner with the goal of cutting down the overall caloric intake in a day. To most people, it may seem unhealthy and damaging to the health, but scientific studies and research has proven that fasting can produce positive results for both the human mind and body. It teaches discipline and fights against unhealthy eating habits. It is a wide umbrella term that is used to define all forms of fasting. This dietary approach does not restrict the intake of specific food items; rather, it works by reducing the overall food intake, leaving enough space to meet the essential body needs. Therefore, it is proven to be far more effective and much easier in implementation, given that the dieter completely understands the nature and science of intermittent fasting.

How to Fast Intermittently?

Intermittent fasting is not one fixed formula for all; rather, it is a flexible regime of calorie restriction. The modified intermittent fasting program is the result of several approaches combined under one head, giving its users a flexible path to adapt according to their particular age, gender, and rates of metabolism. Research on˙ fasting patterns has shown that certain fasting methods are healthier and more beneficial than others. The following are the different methods of intermittent fasting that can be used by women over the age of 50.

1. The Crescendo Method

Having recently surfaced, this method of intermittent fasting was readily adopted by people of all ages and gender. The method has also been proven effective for women over 50, as it sets a practical fasting limit and provides a weekly schedule without limiting the caloric intake. The crescendo method suggests about 12 to 16 hours of fasting, but for only two or three days in a week. That means if a woman chooses a 12-hour limit for the fast, then she can fast for three days in a week and for about two days if the fasting limit is around 16 hours. It is said that these days must be non-consecutive; for example, Friday, Sunday, and Tuesday. The method brings much-needed ease and convenience to all women and does not cause extreme deprivation, weakness, or hunger pangs.

Moreover, the non-consecutive approach provides essential relief to the body and gives constant food breaks.

2. The 5:2 Method

Once you have decided the number of hours, you can select the method of intermittent fasting according to the days. The 5:2 method prescribes the number of days to fast in a week. In this method, a person can fast for two days a week and normally eat during the other five days. The modified 5:2 method also prescribes a caloric limit for two of its fasting days. For women, the caloric intake should not be more than 500 calories on the day of the fast, whereas there is no such restriction for the rest of the five days of the week. This low caloric intake can be easily maintained by having healthy organic food before and after the fast. The two fasting days can be any two days of the week, given that they are non-consecutive. The selection of the days depends on personal preference. For instance, working women can choose to fast on Friday and on the weekend so as not to disrupt their work routine.

3. The Alternate Day Fasting

This method is usually called the "Up-Day, Down-Day Fasting" method, which means that a person needs to fast on the alternating days of the week. It involves one day of fasting, and the next day is specified for eating. When and how to initiate the fast and for how many hours, it depends on personal preference. But the day of fasting must restrict the caloric intake down to 500 calories for women. Ladies! You can maintain this restriction by completely avoiding solid food during the fast while taking low caloric food before and after the fast.

4. Half-Day or 12-Hour Fasting Method

The 12 hours of fast in a day is one of the most balanced approaches and suits people of all body types and work routines. A person can decide himself about the time frame of this 12-hour fast. For example, it can start at 7 pm in the evening and continue till 7 am in the morning. In this way, most of the fasting period is spent during sleep. You can have a meal in the evening then break the fast in the morning with a healthy and rich breakfast. This 12-hour regime is quite suitable for all beginners. If a person chooses this 12-hour program, then it is recommended to fast every other day or on alternate days of the week to achieve weight loss goals and other health benefits.

5. The 16:8 Method

The 16:8 method, also called the lean gain method, shows the ratio of the fasting hours to the hours of the FED state. In this method, a person should fast for 16 hours a day, which gives him an 8-hour period to eat. It depends on the person how many meals to add to this eating period. There can be two or three meals during this time. Such meals need to be rich in content so that they could meet the nutritional needs in a short duration. The 16 hours of fasting seems too difficult to follow, and it is usually not suggested to beginners and those having diabetes. But it is suitable for those who can't fast every other day or who need to quickly achieve their weight loss. Healthy women can surely opt for this method, but most women are suggested to reduce the fasting duration to 15 to 14 hours then gradually move towards the 16 hours method.

6. The 14/10 Method

Since not every woman can comfortably follow the 16:8 intermittent fasting method due to her health concerns, there is yet another method to go for, which is a slight modification of the above-discussed method. In this routine, a woman can fast for 14 hours and eat for 10 hours in a day. This window is enough to satisfy all the energy and caloric needs of the body. To implement this method with ease, start the fast at around even in the evening then break the fast at nine in the morning. This routine is best suited for working women, who can then easily eat food during their work hours.

7. 24 Hours or Eat Stop Eat Method

Some people may describe it as the toughest of all the methods of intermittent fasting, whereas others consider it to be more convenient than fasting every other day. The 24-hour fast seems like a tough job for those who can't endure hunger pangs for too long. It is also hazardous for women suffering from certain nutritional deficiencies, cancer, and diabetes, as it may lead to extremely low levels of glucose in the blood. The method is, however, suitable for people with greater stamina and strength. It is an expert-level fasting method, so a person can switch to this method after a few months of fasting through other methods. Though it is a more rigorous technique, it does save a person from a regular fast. During those 24 hours, you can consume water and zero caloric beverages while avoiding solid food. The fast can extend from one dinner to another, or lunch to lunch or breakfast to breakfast.

In a 24-hour fast, a person must avoid extraneous exercises or intense physical activity to keep the energy levels maintained throughout the fast.

Intermittent Fasting on Keto Diet

Intermittent fasting works best when it is paired with a healthy dietary approach. The ketogenic diet, in this regard, rightly complements the intermittent fasting as it provides a good amount of lasting energy to the dieter during the fast. Carbs are the immediate source of energy that is quickly metabolized and used, whereas fats provide energy through a gradual breakdown, which keeps the dieter energized during the fast. Thus, experts recommend a high fat and a low-carb diet to harness the true benefits of intermittent fasting.

1. Follow the Caloric Limit

Every method of intermittent fasting prescribes a certain caloric limit, which must be taken into consideration while planning a ketogenic meal for fasting day. Reduce the number of calories without compromising on the balanced proportion of both the micro and macronutrients. Take more smoothies and zero caloric juices to keep the caloric intake in check. During the non-fasting days of the week, the meal plan must follow through a balanced approach, which must include small and frequent meals throughout the day.

2. Depend More on Fats

The meal before the fast holds more important! It should be rich with fats so that the body will receive a constant supply of energy throughout the day. Use different sources of fats in one meal to keep a variety of flavors.

3. Slowly Break the Fast

Eating everything at once at the time of breaking the fast is going to reverse the effects of fasting. Even when you are on a ketogenic diet, you must break the fast with a small meal like a smoothie, then take a break and have another small meal. In this way, the excess fats will not be stored in the body.

4. Focus on Hydration

Intermittent fasting does not restrict a person from having zero caloric fluids and water. Since ketogenic lifestyle demands more hydration, a person must constantly consume water during the fast and after it to keep the body hydrated all the time. Muscle and body fatigue can be avoided with active hydration.

5. Make Smart Choices

Since fasting reduces the overall meal consumption during a day or a week, it requires better and healthy food to meet the nutritional needs of the body. A person does not need fillers on this diet; he must consume rich food with a variety of protein sources like meat and seafood along with nuts, oils, and vegetables. Make smarter choices and try to add multiple low-carb ingredients in a single platter to have all the essential nutrients in every meal.

CHAPTER 4: Keto Recipes

BREAKFAST RECIPES

Cheese Crepes

Ingredients

- ➢ 6 ounces cream cheese, softened
- ➢ 1/3 cup Parmesan cheese, grated
- ➢ 6 large organic eggs
- ➢ 1 teaspoon granulated erythritol

- ➤ 1½ tablespoon coconut flour
- ➤ 1/8 teaspoon xanthan gum
- ➤ 2 tablespoons unsalted butter

How to Prepare

1. In a blender, add cream cheese, Parmesan cheese, eggs, and erythritol and pulse on low speed until well combined.
2. While the motor is running, place the coconut flour and xanthan gum and pulse until a thick mixture is formed.
3. Now, pulse on medium speed for a few seconds.
4. Transfer the mixture into a bowl and set aside for about 5 minutes.
5. Divide the mixture into 10 equal-sized portions.
6. In a nonstick pan, melt butter over medium-low heat.
7. Place 1 portion of the mixture and tilt the pan to spread into a thin layer.
8. Cook for about 1½ minutes or until the edges become brown.
9. Flip the crepe and cook for about 15-20 seconds more.
10. Repeat with the remaining mixture.
11. Serve warm with your favorite keto-friendly filling.

Preparation time: 15 minutes

Cooking time: 20 minutes

Total time: 35 minutes

Servings: 5

Nutritional Values

- ➢ *Calories 297*
- ➢ *Net Carbs 1.9 g*
- ➢ *Total Fat 25.1 g*
- ➢ *Saturated Fat 14 g*
- ➢ *Cholesterol 281 mg*
- ➢ *Sodium 391 mg*
- ➢ *Total Carbs 3.5 g*
- ➢ *Fiber 1.6 g*
- ➢ *Sugar 0.5 g*
- ➢ *Protein 13.7 g*

Ricotta Pancakes

Ingredients

> - 4 organic eggs
> - ½ cup ricotta cheese
> - ¼ cup unsweetened vanilla whey protein powder
> - ½ teaspoon organic baking powder
> - Pinch of salt
> - ½ teaspoon liquid stevia
> - 2 tablespoons unsalted butter

How to Prepare

1. In a blender, add all the ingredients and pulse until well combined.
2. In a wok, melt butter over medium heat.

3. Add the desired amount of the mixture and spread it evenly.

4. Cook for about 2–3 minutes or until bottom becomes golden-brown.

5. Flip and cook for about 1–2 minutes or until golden brown.

6. Repeat with the remaining mixture.

7. Serve warm.

Preparation time: 10 minutes

Cooking time: 20 minutes

Total time: 30 minutes

Servings: 4

Nutritional Values

➢ *Calories 184*

➢ *Net Carbs 2.7 g*

➢ *Total Fat 12.9 g*

➢ *Saturated Fat 6.6 g*

➢ *Cholesterol 195 mg*

➢ *Sodium 193 mg*

➢ *Total Carbs 2.7 g*

➢ *Fiber 0 g*

➢ *Sugar 0.8 g*

➢ *Protein 14.6 g*

Yogurt Waffles

Ingredients

- ½ cup golden flax seeds meal
- ½ cup plus 3 tablespoons almond flour
- 1-1½ tablespoons granulated erythritol
- 1 tablespoon unsweetened vanilla whey protein powder
- ¼ teaspoon baking soda
- ½ teaspoon organic baking powder
- ¼ teaspoon xanthan gum
- Salt, as required
- 1 large organic egg, white and yolk separated
- 1 organic whole egg

37

- ➢ 2 tablespoons unsweetened almond milk
- ➢ 1½ tablespoons unsalted butter
- ➢ 3 ounces plain Greek yogurt

How to Prepare

1. Preheat the waffle iron and then grease it.
2. In a large bowl, add the flour, erythritol, protein powder, baking soda, baking powder, xanthan gum, and salt, and mix until well combined.
3. In a second small bowl, add the egg white and beat until stiff peaks form.
4. In a third bowl, add 2 egg yolks, whole egg, almond milk, butter, and yogurt, and beat until well combined.
5. Place egg mixture into the bowl of flour mixture and mix until well combined.
6. Gently, fold in the beaten egg whites.
7. Place ¼ cup of the mixture into preheated waffle iron and cook for about 4–5 minutes or until golden-brown.
8. Repeat with the remaining mixture.
9. Serve warm.

Preparation time: 15 minutes
Cooking time: 25 minutes

Total time: 40 minutes

Servings: 5

Nutritional Values

- ➤ *Calories 250*
- ➤ *Net Carbs 3.2 g*
- ➤ *Total Fat 18.7 g*
- ➤ *Saturated Fat 4 g*
- ➤ *Cholesterol 82 mg*
- ➤ *Sodium 163 mg*
- ➤ *Total Carbs 8.8 g*
- ➤ *Fiber 5.6 g*
- ➤ *Sugar 1.3 g*
- ➤ *Protein 8.4 g*

Broccoli Muffins

Ingredients

- 2 tablespoons unsalted butter
- 6 large organic eggs
- ½ cup heavy whipping cream
- ½ cup Parmesan cheese, grated
- Salt and ground black pepper, as required
- 1¼ cups broccoli, chopped
- 2 tablespoons fresh parsley, chopped
- ½ cup Swiss cheese, grated

How to Prepare

1. Preheat your oven to 350°F.

2. Grease a 12-cup muffin tin.

3. In a bowl, add the eggs, cream, Parmesan cheese, salt, and black pepper, and beat until well combined.

4. Divide the broccoli and parsley in the bottom of each prepared muffin cup evenly.

5. Top with the egg mixture, followed by the Swiss cheese.

6. Bake for about 20 minutes, rotating the pan once halfway through.

7. Remove from the oven and place onto a wire rack for about 5 minutes before serving.

8. Carefully, invert the muffins onto a serving platter and serve warm.

Preparation time: 15 minutes
Cooking time: 20 minutes
Total time: 35 minutes
Servings: 6

Nutritional Values

- ➤ Calories 231
- ➤ Net Carbs 2 g
- ➤ Total Fat 18.1 g
- ➤ Saturated Fat 9.9 g
- ➤ Cholesterol 228 mg
- ➤ Sodium 352 mg
- ➤ Total Carbs 2.5 g
- ➤ Fiber 0.5 g
- ➤ Sugar 0.9 g
- ➤ Protein 13.5 g

Pumpkin Bread

Ingredients

- ➤ 1 2/3 cups almond flour
- ➤ 1½ teaspoons organic baking powder
- ➤ ½ teaspoon pumpkin pie spice
- ➤ ½ teaspoon ground cinnamon
- ➤ ½ teaspoon ground cloves
- ➤ ½ teaspoon salt
- ➤ 8 ounces cream cheese, softened
- ➤ 6 organic eggs, divided
- ➤ 1 tablespoon coconut flour
- ➤ 1 cup powdered erythritol, divided
- ➤ 1 teaspoon stevia powder, divided

- ➤ 1 teaspoon organic lemon extract
- ➤ 1 cup homemade pumpkin puree
- ➤ ½ cup coconut oil, melted

How to Prepare

1. Preheat your oven to 325°F.

2. Lightly, grease 2 bread loaf pans.

3. In a bowl, place almond flour, baking powder, spices, and salt, and mix until well combined.

4. In a second bowl, add the cream cheese, 1 egg, coconut flour, ¼ cup of erythritol, and ¼ teaspoon of the stevia, and with a wire whisk, beat until smooth.

5. In a third bowl, add the pumpkin puree, oil, 5 eggs, ¾ cup of the erythritol and ¾ teaspoon of the stevia and with a wire whisk, beat until well combined.

6. Add the pumpkin mixture into the bowl of the flour mixture and mix until just combined.

7. Place about ¼ of the pumpkin mixture into each loaf pan evenly.

8. Top each pan with the cream cheese mixture evenly, followed by the remaining pumpkin mixture.

9. Bake for about 50–60 minutes or until a toothpick inserted in the center comes out clean.

10. Remove the bread pans from oven and place onto a wire rack to cool for about 10 minutes.

11. Now, invert each bread loaf onto the wire rack to cool completely before slicing.

12. With a sharp knife, cut each bread loaf in the desired-sized slices and serve.

Preparation time: 15 minutes
Cooking time: 1 hour
Total time: 1¼ hours
Servings: 16

Nutritional Values
- *Calories 216*
- *Net Carbs 2.5 g*
- *Total Fat 19.8 g*
- *Saturated Fat 10 g*
- *Cholesterol 77 mg*
- *Sodium 140 mg*
- *Total Carbs 4.5 g*
- *Fiber 2 g*
- *Sugar 1.1 g*
- *Protein 3.4 g*

Eggs in Avocado Cups

Ingredients

- ➢ 2 ripe avocados, halved and pitted
- ➢ 4 organic eggs
- ➢ Salt and ground black pepper, as required
- ➢ 4 tablespoons cheddar cheese, shredded
- ➢ 2 cooked bacon slices, chopped
- ➢ 1 tablespoon scallion greens, chopped

How to Prepare

1. Preheat your oven to 400°F.
2. Carefully, remove abut about 2 tablespoons of flesh from each avocado half.
3. Place avocado halves into a small baking dish.

4. Carefully, crack an egg in each avocado half and sprinkle with salt and black pepper.

5. Top each egg with cheddar cheese evenly.

6. Bake for about 20 minutes or until desired doneness of the eggs.

7. Serve immediately with the garnishing of bacon and chives.

Preparation time: 10 minutes
Cooking time: 20 minutes
Total time: 30 minutes
Servings: 4

Nutritional Values

➢ *Calories 343*
➢ *Net Carbs 2.2 g*
➢ *Total Fat 29.1 g*
➢ *Saturated Fat 9.2 g*
➢ *Cholesterol 186 mg*
➢ *Sodium 372 mg*
➢ *Total Carbs 7.9 g*
➢ *Fiber 5.7 g*
➢ *Sugar 0.8 g*
➢ *Protein 13.8 g*

Cheddar Scramble

Ingredients

- ➤ 2 tablespoons olive oil
- ➤ 1 small yellow onion, chopped finely
- ➤ 12 large organic eggs, beaten lightly
- ➤ Salt and ground black pepper, as required
- ➤ 4 ounces cheddar cheese, shredded

How to Prepare

1. In a large wok, heat oil over medium heat and sauté the onion for about 4–5 minutes.

2. Add the eggs, salt, and black pepper and cook for about 3 minutes, stirring continuously.

3. Remove from the heat and immediately, stir in the cheese.

4. Serve immediately.

Preparation time: 10 minutes
Cooking time: 8 minutes
Total time: 18 minutes
Servings: 6

Nutritional Values

➢ *Calories 264*
➢ *Net Carbs 1.8 g*
➢ *Total Fat 20.9 g*
➢ *Saturated Fat 7.8 g*
➢ *Cholesterol 392 mg*
➢ *Sodium 285 mg*
➢ *Total Carbs 2.1 g*
➢ *Fiber 0.3 g*
➢ *Sugar 1.4 g*
➢ *Protein 17.4 g*

Bacon Omelet

Ingredients

- ➤ 4 large organic eggs
- ➤ 1 tablespoon fresh chives, minced
- ➤ Salt and ground black pepper, as required
- ➤ 4 bacon slices
- ➤ 1 tablespoon unsalted butter
- ➤ 2 ounces cheddar cheese, shredded

How to Prepare

1. In a bowl, add the eggs, chives, salt, and black pepper, and beat until well combined.

2. Heat a non-stick frying pan over medium-high heat and cook the bacon slices for about 8–10 minutes.

3. Place the bacon onto a paper towel-lined plate to drain. Then chop the bacon slices.

4. With paper towels, wipe out the frying pan.

5. In the same frying pan, melt butter over medium-low heat and cook the egg mixture for about 2 minutes.

6. Carefully, flip the omelet and top with chopped bacon.

7. Cook for 1–2 minutes or until desired doneness of eggs.

8. Remove from heat and immediately, place the cheese in the center of omelet.

9. Fold the edges of omelet over cheese and cut into 2 portions.

10. Serve immediately.

Preparation time: 10 minutes
Cooking time: 15 minutes
Total time: 25 minutes
Servings: 2

Nutritional Values

- Calories 427
- Net Carbs 1.2 g
- Total Fat 28.2 g
- Saturated Fat 13.3 g
- Cholesterol 469 mg
- Sodium 668 mg
- Total Carbs 1.2 g
- Fiber 0 g
- Sugar 1 g
- Protein 29.1 g

Green Veggies Quiche

Ingredients

- ➢ 6 organic eggs
- ➢ ½ cup unsweetened almond milk
- ➢ Salt and ground black pepper, as required
- ➢ 2 cups fresh baby spinach, chopped
- ➢ ½ cup green bell pepper, seeded and chopped
- ➢ 1 scallion, chopped
- ➢ ¼ cup fresh cilantro, chopped
- ➢ 1 tablespoon fresh chives, minced
- ➢ 3 tablespoons mozzarella cheese, grated

How to Prepare

1. Preheat your oven to 400°F.

2. Lightly grease a pie dish.

3. In a bowl, add eggs, almond milk, salt, and black pepper, and beat until well combined. Set aside.

4. In another bowl, add the vegetables and herbs and mix well.

5. In the bottom of prepared pie dish, place the veggie mixture evenly and top with the egg mixture.

6. Bake for about 20 minutes or until a wooden skewer inserted in the center comes out clean.

7. Remove pie dish from the oven and immediately sprinkle with the Parmesan cheese.

8. Set aside for about 5 minutes before slicing.

9. Cut into desired sized wedges and serve warm.

Preparation time: 20 minutes

Cooking time: 20 minutes

Total time: 40 minutes

Servings: 4

Nutritional Values

➢ *Calories 176*

- ➢ *Net Carbs 4.1 g*
- ➢ *Total Fat 10.9 g*
- ➢ *Saturated Fat 4.3 g*
- ➢ *Cholesterol 257 mg*
- ➢ *Sodium 296 mg*
- ➢ *Total Carbs 5 g*
- ➢ *Fiber 0.9 g*
- ➢ *Sugar 4 g*
- ➢ *Protein 15.4 g*

Chicken & Asparagus Frittata

Ingredients

- ½ cup grass-fed cooked chicken breast, chopped
- 1/3 cup Parmesan cheese, grated
- 6 organic eggs, beaten lightly
- Salt and ground black pepper, as required
- 1/3 cup boiled asparagus, chopped
- ¼ cup cherry tomatoes, halved
- ¼ cup mozzarella cheese, shredded

How to Prepare

1. Preheat the broiler of oven.

2. In a bowl, add the Parmesan cheese, eggs, salt, and black pepper, and beat until well combined.

3. In a large ovenproof wok, melt butter over medium-high heat and cook the chicken and asparagus for about 2–3 minutes.

4. Add the egg mixture and tomatoes and stir to combine.

5. Cook for about 4–5 minutes.

6. Remove from the heat and sprinkle with the Parmesan cheese.

7. Now, transfer the wok under broiler and broil for about 3–4 minutes or until slightly puffed.

8. Cut into desired sized wedges and serve immediately.

Preparation time: 15 minutes

Cooking time: 12 minutes

Total time: 27 minutes

Servings: 4

Nutritional Values

- Calories 158
- Net Carbs 1.3 g
- Total Fat 9.3 g
- Saturated Fat 3.6 g
- Cholesterol 265 mg
- Sodium 267 mg
- Total Carbs 1.7 g
- Fiber 0.4 g
- Sugar 1 g
- Protein 16.8 g

LUNCH RECIPES

Tuna Burgers

Ingredients

Burgers

- ➤ 1 (15-ounce) can water-packed tuna, drained
- ➤ ½ celery stalk, chopped
- ➤ 2 tablespoon fresh parsley, chopped
- ➤ 1 teaspoon fresh dill, chopped
- ➤ 2 tablespoons walnuts, chopped

- ➢ 2 tablespoons mayonnaise
- ➢ 1 organic egg, beaten
- ➢ 1 tablespoon butter
- ➢ 3 cups lettuce

How to Prepare

1. For burgers: Add all ingredients (except the butter and lettuce) in a bowl and mix until well combined.
2. Make 2 equal-sized patties from mixture.
3. In a frying pan, melt butter over medium heat and cook the patties for about 2–3 minutes.
4. Carefully, flip the side and cook for about 2–3 minutes.
5. Divide the lettuce onto serving plates.
6. Top each plate with 1 burger and serve.

Preparation time: 15 minutes

Cooking time: 6 minutes

Total time: 21 minutes

Servings: 2

Nutritional Values

- ➢ *Calories 631*

- *Net Carbs 2.8 g*
- *Total Fat 39.9 g*
- *Saturated Fat 9.6 g*
- *Cholesterol 168 mg*
- *Sodium 279 mg*
- *Total Carbs 4.1 g*
- *Fiber 0.3 g*
- *Sugar 1.2 g*
- *Protein 61.7 g*

Beef Burgers

Ingredients

- ➤ 8 ounces grass-fed ground beef
- ➤ Salt and ground black pepper, as required
- ➤ 1 ounce mozzarella cheese, cubed
- ➤ 1 tablespoon unsalted butter

Yogurt Sauce

- ➤ 1/3 cup plain Greek yogurt
- ➤ 1 teaspoon fresh lemon juice
- ➤ ¼ teaspoon garlic, minced
- ➤ Salt, as required
- ➤ ½ teaspoon granulated erythritol

How to Prepare

1. In a bowl, add the beef, salt, and black pepper, and mix until well combined.

2. Make 2 equal-sized patties from the mixture.

3. Place mozzarella cube inside of each patty and cover with the beef.

4. In a frying pan, melt butter over medium heat and cook the patties for about 2–3 minutes per side.

5. Divide the greens onto serving plates and top each with 1 patty.

6. Serve immediately.

7. Meanwhile, for the yogurt sauce: place all the ingredients in a serving bowl and mix until well combined.

8. Divide patties onto each serving plate and serve alongside the yogurt sauce.

Preparation time: 15 minutes

Cooking time: 6 minutes

Total time: 21 minutes

Servings: 2

Nutritional Values

- ➢ Calories 322
- ➢ Net Carbs 3.5 g
- ➢ Total Fat 19.8 g
- ➢ Saturated Fat 10.1 g
- ➢ Cholesterol 100 mg
- ➢ Sodium 308 mg
- ➢ Total Carbs 3.5 g
- ➢ Fiber 0 g
- ➢ Sugar 2.9 g
- ➢ Protein 29.5 g

Lamb Meatballs

Ingredients

Tomato Chutney

- ➢ 2 cups tomatoes, chopped
- ➢ 2 tablespoons fresh red chili, chopped
- ➢ 1 tablespoon fresh ginger, peeled and chopped
- ➢ ½ tablespoon fresh lime zest, grated
- ➢ ¼ cup organic apple cider vinegar
- ➢ 2 tablespoons red boat fish sauce
- ➢ 1 tablespoon fresh lime juice
- ➢ 2 tablespoons granulated erythritol
- ➢ ¼ teaspoon mustard powder

- ➢ ½ teaspoon dehydrated onion flakes
- ➢ ½ teaspoon ground coriander
- ➢ ½ teaspoon ground cinnamon
- ➢ ¼ teaspoon ground allspice
- ➢ 1/8 teaspoon ground cloves
- ➢ Salt, as required

Meatballs

- ➢ 1 pound grass-fed ground lamb
- ➢ 1 tablespoon olive oil
- ➢ 1 teaspoon dehydrated onion flakes, crushed
- ➢ ½ teaspoon granulated garlic
- ➢ ½ teaspoon ground cumin
- ➢ ½ teaspoon red pepper flakes, crushed
- ➢ Salt, as required

How to Prepare

1. For chutney: Add all the ingredients in a pan over medium heat (except for cilantro) and bring to a boil.
2. Adjust the heat to low and simmer for about 45 minutes, stirring occasionally.
3. Remove from heat and set aside to cool.
4. Meanwhile, preheat your oven to 400°F.
5. Line a larger baking sheet with parchment paper.

6. For meatballs: In a large bowl, place all the ingredients and with your hands, mix until well combined.

7. Shape the mixture into desired and equal-sized balls.

8. Arrange meatballs into the prepared baking sheet in a single layer and bake for about 15–20 minutes or until done completely.

9. Serve the meatballs with chutney.

Preparation time: 20 minutes
Cooking time: 1 hour 10 minutes
Total time: 1½ hours
Servings: 6

Nutritional Values

➢ *Calories 184*
➢ *Net Carbs 2.5 g*
➢ *Total Fat 8.1 g*
➢ *Saturated Fat 2.3 g*
➢ *Cholesterol 68 mg*
➢ *Sodium 586 mg*
➢ *Total Carbs 3.5 g*
➢ *Fiber 1 g*
➢ *Sugar 1.9 g*
➢ *Protein 23.3 g*

Stuffed Zucchini

Ingredients

- ➤ 4 medium zucchinis, halved lengthwise
- ➤ 1 cup red bell pepper, seeded and minced
- ➤ ½ cup Kalamata olives, pitted and minced
- ➤ ½ cup fresh tomatoes, minced
- ➤ 1 teaspoon garlic, minced
- ➤ 1 tablespoon dried oregano, crushed
- ➤ Salt and ground black pepper, as required
- ➤ ½ cup feta cheese, crumbled

How to Prepare

1. Preheat your oven to 350°F.

2. Grease a large baking sheet.

3. With a melon baller, scoop out the flesh of each zucchini half. Discard the flesh.

4. In a bowl, mix together the bell pepper, olives, tomatoes, garlic, oregano, salt, and black pepper.

5. Stuff each zucchini half with the veggie mixture evenly.

6. Arrange zucchini halves onto the prepared baking sheet and bake for about 15 minutes.

7. Now, set the oven to broiler on high.

8. Top each zucchini half with feta cheese and broil for about 3 minutes.

9. Serve hot.

Preparation time: 15 minutes
Cooking time: 18 minutes
Total time: 33 minutes
Servings: 8

Nutritional Values

➢ *Calories 59*
➢ *Net Carbs 4.3 g*

- *Total Fat 3.2 g*
- *Saturated Fat 1.6 g*
- *Cholesterol 8 mg*
- *Sodium 208 mg*
- *Total Carbs 6.2 g*
- *Fiber 0.9 g*
- *Sugar 3.2 g*
- *Protein 2.9 g*

Stuffed Bell Peppers

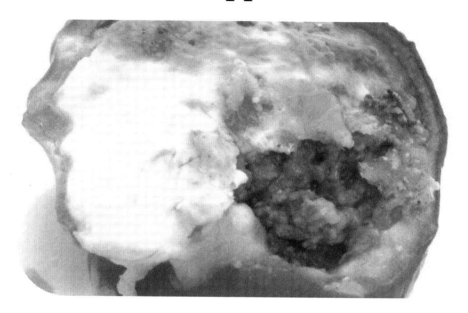

Ingredients

- ➤ 2 teaspoons coconut oil
- ➤ 1 pound grass-fed ground beef
- ➤ 1 garlic clove, minced
- ➤ 1 cup white mushrooms, chopped
- ➤ 1 cup yellow onion, chopped
- ➤ Salt and ground black pepper, as required
- ➤ ½ cup homemade tomato puree
- ➤ 3 large green bell peppers, halved lengthwise and cored
- ➤ 1 cup water
- ➤ 4 ounces sharp cheddar cheese, shredded

How to Prepare

1. Melt the coconut oil in a wok over medium-high heat and sauté the garlic for about 30 seconds.

2. Add the beef and cook for about 5 minutes, crumbling with the spoon.

3. Add the mushrooms and onion and cook for about 5–6 minutes.

4. Stir in salt and black pepper and cook for about 30 seconds.

5. Remove from the heat and stir in tomato puree.

6. Meanwhile, in a microwave-safe dish, arrange the bell peppers, cut-side down.

7. Pour the water in baking dish.

8. With a plastic wrap, cover the baking dish and microwave on high for about 4–5 minutes.

9. Remove from microwave and uncover the baking dish.

10. Dain the water completely.

11. Now in the baking dish, arrange the bell peppers, cut-side up.

12. Stuff the bell peppers evenly with beef mixture and top with cheese.

13. Microwave on High for about 2–3 minutes.

14. Serve warm.

Preparation time: 15 minutes

Cooking time: 20 minutes

Total time: 35 minutes

Servings: 6

Nutritional Values

- ➢ *Calories 258*
- ➢ *Net Carbs 5.7 g*
- ➢ *Total Fat 15.4 g*
- ➢ *Saturated Fat 8.4 g*
- ➢ *Cholesterol 70 mg*
- ➢ *Sodium 206 mg*
- ➢ *Total Carbs 8 g*
- ➢ *Fiber 2.3 g*
- ➢ *Sugar 4.1 g*
- ➢ *Protein 21.8 g*

Spinach in Creamy Sauce

Ingredients

- ➤ 2 tablespoons unsalted butter
- ➤ 1 small yellow onion, chopped
- ➤ 1 cup cream cheese, softened
- ➤ 2 (10-ounce) packages frozen spinach, thawed and squeezed dry
- ➤ 2–3 tablespoons water
- ➤ Salt and ground black pepper, as required
- ➤ 1 teaspoon fresh lemon juice

How to Prepare

1. Melt the butter in a wok over medium heat and sauté the onion for about 6–8 minutes.

2. Add the cream cheese and cook for about 2 minutes or until melted completely.

3. Stir in the spinach and water and cook for about 4–5 minutes.

4. Stir in the salt, black pepper, and lemon juice, and remove from heat.

5. Serve immediately.

Preparation time: 10 minutes
Cooking time: 15 minutes
Total time: 25 minutes
Servings: 4

Nutritional Values

> *Calories 293*
> *Net Carbs 4.9 g*
> *Total Fat 26.6 g*
> *Saturated Fat 16.5 g*
> *Cholesterol 79 mg*
> *Sodium 364 mg*
> *Total Carbs 8.4 g*
> *Fiber 3.5 g*
> *Sugar 1.5 g*
> *Protein 8.7 g*

Creamy Zucchini Noodles

Ingredients

- 1¼ cups heavy whipping cream
- ¼ cup mayonnaise
- Salt and ground black pepper, as required
- 30 ounces zucchini, spiralized with blade C
- 3 ounces Parmesan cheese, grated
- 2 tablespoons fresh mint leaves
- 2 tablespoons butter, melted

How to Prepare

1. In a pan, add the heavy cream and bring to a boil.
2. Lower the heat to low and cook until reduced in half.

3. Add the mayonnaise, salt, and black pepper and cook until mixture is warm enough.

4. Add the zucchini noodles and gently, stir to combine.

5. Stir in the Parmesan cheese and immediately, remove from the heat.

6. Divide the zucchini noodles onto 4 serving plates and immediately, drizzle with the melted butter.

7. Serve immediately.

Preparation time: 15 minutes
Cooking time: 10 minutes
Total time: 25 minutes
Servings: 6

Nutritional Values

➢ *Calories 249*
➢ *Net Carbs 4.4 g*
➢ *Total Fat 23.1 g*
➢ *Saturated Fat 11.3 g*
➢ *Cholesterol 58 mg*
➢ *Sodium 270 mg*
➢ *Total Carbs 6.1 g*
➢ *Fiber 1.7 g*
➢ *Sugar 2.5 g*
➢ *Protein 6.9 g*

Broccoli with Bell Peppers

Ingredients

- ➤ 2 tablespoons butter
- ➤ 2 garlic cloves, minced
- ➤ 1 large yellow onion, sliced
- ➤ 3 large red bell peppers, seeded and thinly sliced
- ➤ 2 cups small broccoli florets
- ➤ 1 tablespoon low-sodium soy sauce
- ➤ ¼ cup homemade vegetable broth
- ➤ Ground black pepper, as required

How to Prepare

1. In a large wok, melt butter oil over medium heat and sauté the garlic for about 1 minute.

2. Add the vegetables and stir fry for about 5 minutes.

3. Stir in the broth and soy sauce and stir fry for about 4 minutes or until the desired doneness of the vegetables.

4. Stir in the black pepper and remove from the heat.

5. Serve hot.

Preparation time: 15 minutes

Cooking time: 10 minutes

Total time: 25 minutes

Servings: 6

Nutritional Values

➢ *Calories 74*

➢ *Net Carbs 5.8 g*

➢ *Total Fat 4.1 g*

➢ *Saturated Fat 2.5 g*

➢ *Cholesterol 10 mg*

➢ *Sodium 163 mg*

➢ *Total Carbs 8.6 g*

➢ *Fiber 2.8 g*

➢ *Sugar 3.7 g*

➢ *Protein 2.1 g*

Shrimp in Cream Sauce

Ingredients

Shrimp

- ➤ ½ ounce Parmigiano Reggiano cheese, grated
- ➤ 1 large organic egg
- ➤ 2 tablespoons almond flour
- ➤ ½ teaspoon organic baking powder
- ➤ ¼ teaspoon curry powder
- ➤ 1 tablespoon water
- ➤ 1 pound shrimp, peeled and deveined
- ➤ 3 tablespoons unsalted butter

Creamy Sauce

- ➢ 2 tablespoons unsalted butter
- ➢ ½ of small yellow onion, chopped
- ➢ 1 garlic clove, finely chopped
- ➢ ½ cup heavy cream
- ➢ 1/3 cup cheddar cheese, grated
- ➢ 2 tablespoons fresh parsley, chopped
- ➢ Salt and ground black pepper, as required

How to Prepare

1. For shrimp: Add all the ingredients (except shrimp) and butter in a bowl and mix until well combined.

2. Add the shrimp and coat with cheese mixture generously.

3. Melt the butter in a pan over medium heat and stir fry the shrimp for about 3–4 minutes or until golden-brown from all sides.

4. With a slotted spoon, transfer the shrimp onto a plate.

5. For sauce: Melt the butter in another pan over medium-low heat and sauté the onion for about 3–5 minutes.

6. Add garlic and sauté for about 1 minute.

7. Reduce the heat to low and stir in heavy cream and cheddar until well combined.

8. Cook for about 1–2 minutes, stirring continuously.

9. Stir in the cooked shrimps, parsley, salt, and black pepper, and cook for about 1–2 minutes.

10. Remove the pan of shrimp mixture from heat and transfer onto the serving plates.

11. Serve hot.

Preparation time: 20 minutes

Cooking time: 15 minutes

Total time: 25 minutes

Servings: 4

Nutritional Values

➢ *Calories 410*

➢ *Net Carbs 4 g*

➢ *Total Fat 29.1 g*

➢ *Saturated Fat 16.4 g*

➢ *Cholesterol 357 mg*

➢ *Sodium 523 mg*

➢ *Total Carbs 4.7 g*

➢ *Fiber 0.7 g*

➢ *Sugar 0.7 g*

➢ *Protein 32.6 g*

Scallops in Garlic Sauce

Ingredients

- ➤ 1¼ pounds fresh sea scallops, side muscles removed
- ➤ Salt and ground black pepper, as required
- ➤ 4 tablespoons butter, divided
- ➤ 5 garlic cloves, chopped
- ➤ ¼ cup homemade chicken broth
- ➤ 1 cup heavy cream
- ➤ 1 tablespoon fresh lemon juice
- ➤ 2 tablespoons fresh parsley, chopped

How to Prepare

1. Sprinkle the scallops evenly with salt and black pepper.
2. Melt 2 tablespoons of butter in a large pan over medium-high heat and cook the scallops for about 2–3 minutes per side.
3. Flip the scallops and cook for about 2 more minutes.
4. With a slotted spoon, transfer the scallops onto a plate.
5. Now, melt the remaining butter in the same pan over medium heat and sauté the garlic for about 1 minute.
6. Pour the broth and bring to a gentle boil.
7. Cook for about 2 minutes.
8. Stir in the cream and cook for about 1–2 minutes or until slightly thickened.
9. Stir in the cooked scallops and lemon juice and remove from heat.
10. Garnish with fresh parsley and serve hot.

Preparation time: 15 minutes
Cooking time: 13 minutes
Total time: 28 minutes
Servings: 4

Nutritional Values

- ➤ Calories 435
- ➤ Net Carbs 4.6 g
- ➤ Total Fat 32.7 g
- ➤ Saturated Fat 21.4 g
- ➤ Cholesterol 157 mg
- ➤ Sodium 398 mg
- ➤ Total Carbs 4.7 g
- ➤ Fiber 0.1 g
- ➤ Sugar 0.1 g
- ➤ Protein 24.5 g

DINNER RECIPES

Roasted Cornish Hen

Ingredients

- ➢ 1 tablespoon dried basil, crushed
- ➢ 2 tablespoons lemon pepper
- ➢ 1 tablespoon poultry seasoning
- ➢ Salt, as required
- ➢ 4 (1½-pound) Cornish game hens, rinsed and dried completely
- ➢ 2 tablespoons olive oil

- ➢ 1 yellow onion, chopped
- ➢ 1 celery stalk, chopped
- ➢ 1 green bell pepper, seeded and chopped

How to Prepare

1. Preheat your oven to 375°F. Arrange lightly greased racks in 2 large roasting pans.
2. In a bowl, mix well basil, lemon pepper, poultry seasoning, and salt.
3. Coat each hen with oil and then, rub evenly with the seasoning mixture.
4. In a next bowl, mix together the onion, celery, and bell pepper.
5. Stuff the cavity of each hen loosely with veggie mixture.
6. Arrange the hens into prepared roasting pans, keeping plenty of space between them.
7. Roast for about 60 minutes or until the juices run clear.
8. Remove the hens from oven and place onto a cutting board.
9. With a foil piece, cover each hen loosely for about 10 minutes before carving.
10. Cut into desired size pieces and serve.

Preparation time: 15 minutes

Cooking time: 1 hour

Total time: 1¼ hours

Servings: 8

Nutritional Values

- ➤ Calories 714
- ➤ Net Carbs 2.8 g
- ➤ Total Fat 52.2 g
- ➤ Saturated Fat 0.5g
- ➤ Cholesterol 349 mg
- ➤ Sodium 235 mg
- ➤ Total Carbs 3.8 g
- ➤ Fiber 1 g
- ➤ Sugar 1.4 g
- ➤ Protein 58.2 g

Butter Chicken

Ingredients

- ➢ 3 tablespoons unsalted butter
- ➢ 1 medium yellow onion, chopped
- ➢ 2 garlic cloves, minced
- ➢ 1 teaspoon fresh ginger, minced
- ➢ 1½ pounds grass-fed chicken breasts, cut into ¾-inch chunks
- ➢ 2 tomatoes, chopped finely
- ➢ 1 tablespoon garam masala
- ➢ 1 teaspoon red chili powder

- ➤ 1 teaspoon ground cumin
- ➤ Salt and ground black pepper, as required
- ➤ 1 cup heavy cream
- ➤ 2 tablespoons fresh cilantro, chopped

How to Prepare

1. Melt butter in a large wok over medium-high heat and sauté the onions for about 5–6 minutes.

2. Now, add in ginger and garlic and sauté for about 1 minute.

3. Add the tomatoes and cook for about 2–3 minutes, crushing with the back of spoon.

4. Stir in the chicken spices, salt, and black pepper, and cook for about 6–8 minutes or until desired doneness of the chicken.

5. Stir in the heavy cream and cook for about 8–10 more minutes, stirring occasionally.

6. Garnish with fresh cilantro and serve hot.

Preparation time: 15 minutes
Cooking time: 28 minutes
Total time: 43 minutes
Servings: 5

Nutritional Values

- Calories 507
- Net Carbs 4 g
- Total Fat 33.4 g
- Saturated Fat 18.6 g
- Cholesterol 203 mg
- Sodium 211 mg
- Total Carbs 5.5 g
- Fiber 1.5 g
- Sugar 2.3 g
- Protein 40.5 g

Chicken & Broccoli Casserole

Ingredients

- ➤ 2 tablespoons butter
- ➤ ¼ cup cooked bacon, crumbled
- ➤ 2½ cups cheddar cheese, shredded and divided
- ➤ 4 ounces cream cheese, softened
- ➤ ¼ cup heavy whipping cream
- ➤ ½ pack ranch seasoning mix
- ➤ 2/3 cup homemade chicken broth
- ➤ 1½ cups small broccoli florets
- ➤ 2 cups cooked grass-fed chicken breast, shredded

How to Prepare

1. Preheat your oven to 350°F.

2. Arrange a rack in the upper portion of the oven.

3. For chicken mixture: In a large wok, melt the butter over low heat.

4. Add the bacon, ½ cup of cheddar cheese, cream cheese, heavy whipping cream, ranch seasoning, and broth, and with a wire whisk, beat until well combined.

5. Cook for about 5 minutes, stirring frequently.

6. Meanwhile, in a microwave-safe dish, place the broccoli and microwave until desired tenderness is achieved.

7. In the wok, add the chicken and broccoli and mix until well combined.

8. Remove from the heat and transfer the mixture into a casserole dish.

9. Top the chicken mixture with the remaining cheddar cheese.

10. Bake for about 25 minutes.

11. Now, set the oven to broiler.

12. Broil the chicken mixture for about 2–3 minutes or until cheese is bubbly.

13. Serve hot.

Preparation time: 15 minutes

Cooking time: 35 minutes

Total time: 50 minutes

Servings: 6

Nutritional Values

> ➢ *Calories 449*
> ➢ *Net Carbs 2.3 g*
> ➢ *Total Fat 33.5 g*
> ➢ *Saturated Fat 20.1 g*
> ➢ *Cholesterol 133 mg*
> ➢ *Sodium 1001 mg*
> ➢ *Total Carbs 2.9 g*
> ➢ *Fiber 0.6 g*
> ➢ *Sugar 0.8 g*
> ➢ *Protein 31.3 g*

Turkey Chili

Ingredients

- ➤ 2 tablespoons olive oil
- ➤ 1 small yellow onion, chopped
- ➤ 1 green bell pepper, seeded and chopped
- ➤ 4 garlic cloves, minced
- ➤ 1 jalapeño pepper, chopped
- ➤ 1 teaspoon dried thyme, crushed
- ➤ 2 tablespoons red chili powder
- ➤ 1 tablespoon ground cumin
- ➤ 2 pounds lean ground turkey

- ➤ 2 cups fresh tomatoes, chopped finely
- ➤ 2 ounces sugar-free tomato paste
- ➤ 2 cups homemade chicken broth
- ➤ 1 cup water
- ➤ Salt and ground black pepper, as required
- ➤ 1 cup cheddar cheese, shredded

How to Prepare

1. In a large Dutch oven, heat oil over medium heat and sauté the onion and bell pepper for about 5–7 minutes.
2. Add the garlic, jalapeño pepper, thyme, and spices and sauté for about 1 minute.
3. Add the turkey and cook for about 4–5 minutes.
4. Stir in the tomatoes, tomato paste, and cacao powder, and cook for about 2 minutes.
5. Add in the broth and water and bring to a boil.
6. Now, reduce the heat to low and simmer, covered for about 2 hours.
7. Add in salt and black pepper and remove from the heat.
8. Top with cheddar cheese and serve hot.

Preparation time: 15 minutes
Cooking time: 2¼ hours

Total time: 2½ hours

Servings: 8

Nutritional Values

- ➢ *Calories 234*
- ➢ *Net Carbs 4.8 g*
- ➢ *Total Fat 12.6 g*
- ➢ *Saturated Fat 3.2 g*
- ➢ *Cholesterol 81 mg*
- ➢ *Sodium 328 mg*
- ➢ *Total Carbs 6.9 g*
- ➢ *Fiber 2.1 g*
- ➢ *Sugar 3.2 g*
- ➢ *Protein 24.9 g*

Beef Curry

Ingredients

- ➤ 2 tablespoons butter
- ➤ 2 tomatoes, chopped finely
- ➤ 2 tablespoons curry powder
- ➤ 2½ cups unsweetened coconut milk
- ➤ ½ cup homemade chicken broth
- ➤ 2½ pounds grass-fed beef chuck roast, cubed into 1-inch size
- ➤ Salt and ground black pepper, as required
- ➤ ¼ cup fresh cilantro, chopped

How to Prepare

1. Melt butter in a large pan over low heat and cook the tomatoes and curry powder for about 3–4 minutes, crushing the tomatoes with the back of spoon.

2. Stir in the coconut milk, and broth, and bring to a gentle simmer, stirring occasionally.

3. Simmer for about 4–5 minutes.

4. Stir in beef and bring to a boil over medium heat.

5. Adjust the heat to low and cook, covered for about 2½ hours, stirring occasionally

6. Remove from heat and with a slotted spoon, transfer the beef into a bowl.

7. Set the pan of curry aside for about 10 minutes.

8. With a slotted spoon, remove the fats from top of curry.

9. Return the pan over medium heat.

10. Stir in the cooked beef and bring to a gentle simmer.

11. Adjust the heat to low and cook, uncovered for about 30 minutes or until desired thickness.

12. Stir in salt and black pepper and remove from the heat.

13. Garnish with fresh cilantro and serve hot.

Preparation time: 10 minutes

Cooking time: 3¼ hours

Total time: 3 hours 25 minutes

Servings: 8

Nutritional Values

- ➢ *Calories 666*
- ➢ *Net Carbs 3.2 g*
- ➢ *Total Fat 53 g*
- ➢ *Saturated Fat 27 g*
- ➢ *Cholesterol 154 mg*
- ➢ *Sodium 204 mg*
- ➢ *Total Carbs 4.1 g*
- ➢ *Fiber 0.9 g*
- ➢ *Sugar 2.8 g*
- ➢ *Protein 38.8 g*

Shepherd's Pie

Ingredients

- ➤ ¼ cup olive oil
- ➤ 1 pound grass-fed ground beef
- ➤ ½ cup celery, chopped
- ➤ ¼ cup yellow onion, chopped
- ➤ 3 garlic cloves, minced
- ➤ 1 cup tomatoes, chopped
- ➤ 2 (12-ounce) packages riced cauliflower, cooked and well drained
- ➤ 1 cup cheddar cheese, shredded
- ➤ ¼ cup Parmesan cheese, shredded
- ➤ 1 cup heavy cream

➢ 1 teaspoon dried thyme

How to Prepare

1. Preheat your oven to 350°F.
2. Heat oil in a large nonstick wok over medium heat and cook the ground beef, celery, onions, and garlic for about 8–10 minutes.
3. Remove from the heat and drain the excess grease.
4. Immediately stir in the tomatoes.
5. Transfer mixture into a 10x7-inch casserole dish evenly.
6. In a food processor, add the cauliflower, cheeses, cream, and thyme, and pulse until a mashed potatoes-like mixture is formed.
7. Spread the cauliflower mixture over the meat in the casserole dish evenly.
8. Bake for about 35–40 minutes.
9. Remove casserole dish from oven and let it cool slightly before serving.
10. Cut into desired sized pieces and serve.

Preparation time: 20 minutes
Cooking time: 50 minutes
Total time: 1 hour 10 minutes
Servings: 6

Nutritional Values

- Calories 404
- Net Carbs 5.7 g
- Total Fat 30.5 g
- Saturated Fat 13.4 g
- Cholesterol 100 mg
- Sodium 274 mg
- Total Carbs 9.2 g
- Fiber 3.5 g
- Sugar 4 g
- Protein 24.5 g

Meatballs Curry

Ingredients

Meatballs

- ➢ 1 pound lean ground pork
- ➢ 2 organic eggs, beaten
- ➢ 3 tablespoons yellow onion, finely chopped
- ➢ ¼ cup fresh parsley leaves, chopped
- ➢ ¼ teaspoon fresh ginger, minced
- ➢ 2 garlic cloves, minced
- ➢ 1 jalapeño pepper, seeded and finely chopped
- ➢ 1 teaspoon granulated erythritol
- ➢ 1 teaspoon curry powder

> 3 tablespoons olive oil

Curry

> 1 yellow onion, chopped
> Salt, as required
> 2 garlic cloves, minced
> ¼ teaspoon fresh ginger, minced
> 1 tablespoon curry powder
> 1 (14-ounce) can unsweetened coconut milk
> Ground black pepper, as required
> ¼ cup fresh parsley, minced

How to Prepare

1. For meatballs: Place all the ingredients (except oil) in a large bowl and mix until well combined.

2. Make small-sized balls from the mixture.

3. Heat the oil in a large wok over medium heat and cook meatballs for about 3–5 minutes or until golden-brown from all sides.

4. Transfer the meatballs into a bowl.

5. For curry: In the same wok, add onion and a pinch of salt, and sauté for about 4–5 minutes.

6. Add the garlic and ginger, and sauté for about 1 minute.

7. Add the curry powder and sauté for about 1–2 minutes.

8. Add coconut milk and meatballs, and bring to a gentle simmer.

9. Adjust the heat to low and simmer, covered for about 10–12 minutes.

10. Season with salt and black pepper and remove from the heat.

11. Top with parsley and serve.

Preparation time: 15 minutes
Cooking time: 25 minutes
Total time: 40 minutes
Servings: 6

Nutritional Values

- ➢ *Calories 350*
- ➢ *Net Carbs 4.2 g*
- ➢ *Total Fat 29.1 g*
- ➢ *Saturated Fat 9.7 g*
- ➢ *Cholesterol 55 mg*
- ➢ *Sodium 73 mg*
- ➢ *Total Carbs 5.2 g*
- ➢ *Fiber 1 g*
- ➢ *Sugar 2.7 g*
- ➢ *Protein 16.2 g*

Pork with Veggies

Ingredients

- ➤ 1 pound pork loin, cut into thin strips
- ➤ 2 tablespoons olive oil, divided
- ➤ 1 teaspoon garlic, minced
- ➤ 1 teaspoon fresh ginger, minced
- ➤ 2 tablespoons low-sodium soy sauce
- ➤ 1 tablespoon fresh lemon juice
- ➤ 1 teaspoon sesame oil
- ➤ 1 tablespoon granulated erythritol
- ➤ 1 teaspoon arrowroot starch
- ➤ 10 ounces broccoli florets
- ➤ 1 carrot, peeled and sliced

> 1 large red bell pepper, seeded and cut into strips
> 2 scallions, cut into 2-inch pieces

How to Prepare

1. In a bowl, mix well pork strips, ½ tablespoon of olive oil, garlic, and ginger.

2. For sauce: Add the soy sauce, lemon juice, sesame oil, Swerve, and arrowroot starch in a small bowl and mix well.

3. Heat the remaining olive oil in a large nonstick wok over high heat and sear the pork strips for about 3–4 minutes or until cooked through.

4. With a slotted spoon, transfer the pork into a bowl.

5. In the same wok, add the carrot and cook for about 2–3 minutes.

6. Add the broccoli, bell pepper, and scallion, and cook, covered for about 1–2 minutes.

7. Stir the cooked pork, sauce, and stir fry, and cook for about 3–5 minutes or until desired doneness, stirring occasionally.

8. Remove from the heat and serve.

Preparation time: 15 minutes
Cooking time: 15 minutes

Total time: 30 minutes

Servings: 5

Nutritional Values

- ➤ *Calories 315*
- ➤ *Net Carbs 5.7 g*
- ➤ *Total Fat 19.4 g*
- ➤ *Saturated Fat 5.7 g*
- ➤ *Cholesterol 73 mg*
- ➤ *Sodium 438 mg*
- ➤ *Total Carbs 8.3 g*
- ➤ *Fiber 2.6 g*
- ➤ *Sugar 3 g*
- ➤ *Protein 27.4 g*

Pork Taco Bake

Ingredients

Crust

- ➢ 3 organic eggs
- ➢ 4 ounces cream cheese, softened
- ➢ ½ teaspoon taco seasoning
- ➢ 1/3 cup heavy cream
- ➢ 8 ounces cheddar cheese, shredded

Topping

- ➢ 1 pound lean ground pork
- ➢ 4 ounces canned chopped green chilies

- ¼ cup sugar-free tomato sauce
- 3 teaspoons taco seasoning
- 8 ounces cheddar cheese, shredded
- ¼ cup fresh basil leaves

How to Prepare

1. Preheat your oven to 375°F.
2. Lightly grease a 13x9-inch baking dish.
3. For crust: In a bowl, add the eggs and cream cheese, and beat until well combined and smooth.
4. Add the taco seasoning and heavy cream, and mix well.
5. Place cheddar cheese evenly in the bottom of prepared baking dish.
6. Spread cream cheese mixture evenly over cheese.
7. Bake for about 25–30 minutes.
8. Remove baking dish from the oven and set aside for about 5 minutes.
9. Meanwhile, for the topping: Heat a large nonstick wok over medium-high heat and cook the pork for about 8–10 minutes.
10. Drain the excess grease from wok.
11. Stir in the green chilies, tomato sauce, and taco seasoning, and remove from the heat.

12. Place the pork mixture evenly over crust and sprinkle with cheese.

13. Bake for about 18–20 minutes or until bubbly.

14. Remove from the oven and set aside for about 5 minutes.

15. Cut into desired size slices and serve with the garnishing of basil leaves.

Preparation time: 15 minutes

Cooking time: 1 hour

Total time: 1¼ hours

Servings: 6

Nutritional Values

- ➢ *Calories 547*
- ➢ *Net Carbs 4.1 g*
- ➢ *Total Fat 39 g*
- ➢ *Saturated Fat 23.2 g*
- ➢ *Cholesterol 264 mg*
- ➢ *Sodium 870 mg*
- ➢ *Total Carbs 4.6 g*
- ➢ *Fiber 0.5 g*
- ➢ *Sugar 1.4 g*
- ➢ *Protein 43.2 g*

Spinach Pie

Ingredients

- ➤ 2 tablespoons butter, divided
- ➤ 2 tablespoons yellow onion, chopped
- ➤ 1 (16-ounce) bag frozen chopped spinach, thawed and squeezed
- ➤ 1½ cups heavy cream
- ➤ 3 organic eggs
- ➤ ½ teaspoon ground nutmeg
- ➤ Salt and ground black pepper, as required
- ➤ ½ cup Swiss cheese, shredded

How to Prepare

1. Preheat your oven to 375°F.

2. Grease a 9-inch baking dish.

3. In a large wok, melt 1 tablespoon of butter over medium-high heat and sauté onion for about 4–5 minutes.

4. Add spinach and cook for about 2–3 minutes or until all the liquid is absorbed.

5. In a bowl add cream, eggs, nutmeg, salt, and black pepper, and beat until well combined.

6. Transfer the spinach mixture in the bottom of prepared baking dish evenly.

7. Place the egg mixture over spinach mixture evenly and sprinkle with cheese.

8. Top with remaining butter in the shape of dots at many places.

9. Bake for about 25–30 minutes or until top becomes golden-brown.

10. Serve warm.

Preparation time: 15 minutes
Cooking time: 38 minutes
Total time: 53 minutes
Servings: 5

Nutritional Values

- Calories 267
- Net Carbs 0 g
- Total Fat 24 g
- Saturated Fat 14.1 g
- Cholesterol 170 mg
- Sodium 207 mg
- Total Carbs 5.6 g
- Fiber 2.1 g
- Sugar 1 g
- Protein 9.7 g

POULTRY RECIPES

Grilled Whole Chicken

Ingredients

- ¼ cup butter, melted
- 2 tablespoons fresh lemon juice
- 2 teaspoons fresh lemon zest, grated finely
- 1 teaspoon dried oregano, crushed
- 2 teaspoons paprika
- 1 teaspoon onion powder
- 1 teaspoon garlic powder
- Salt and ground black pepper, as required

➤ 1 (4-pound) grass-fed whole chicken, neck and giblets removed

How to Prepare

1. Preheat the grill to medium heat. Grease the grill grate.

2. In a bowl, add the butter, lemon juice, lemon zest, oregano, spices, salt, and black pepper, and mix until well combined.

3. Place chicken onto a large cutting board, breast-side down.

4. With a sharp knife, cut along both sides of backbone and then remove the backbone.

5. Now, flip the breast side of chicken up and open it like a book.

6. With the palm of your hands, firmly press breast to flatten.

7. Coat the whole chicken with the oil mixture generously.

8. Arrange the chicken onto the grill and cook for about 16–20 minutes, flipping once halfway through.

9. Remove from the grill and place the chicken onto a cutting board for about 5–10 minutes before carving.

10. With a sharp knife, cut the chicken into desired-sized pieces and serve.

Preparation time: 20 minutes
Cooking time: 20 minutes
Total time: 40 minutes
Servings: 6

Nutritional Values

- ➢ *Calories 532*
- ➢ *Net Carbs 0 g*
- ➢ *Total Fat 17 g*
- ➢ *Saturated Fat 7.5 g*
- ➢ *Cholesterol 253 mg*
- ➢ *Sodium 274 mg*
- ➢ *Total Carbs 1.5 g*
- ➢ *Fiber 0.5 g*
- ➢ *Sugar 0.5 g*
- ➢ *Protein 88 g*

Grilled Chicken Breast

Ingredients

- ➢ ¼ cup balsamic vinegar
- ➢ 2 tablespoons olive oil
- ➢ 1½ teaspoons fresh lemon juice
- ➢ ½ teaspoon lemon-pepper seasoning
- ➢ 4 (6-ounce) grass-fed boneless skinless chicken breast halves, pounded slightly

How to Prepare

1. In a glass baking dish, place the vinegar, oil, lemon juice, and seasoning, and mix well.
2. Add the chicken breasts and coat with the mixture generously.

3. Refrigerate to marinate for about 25–30 minutes.

4. Preheat the grill to medium heat. Grease the grill grate.

5. Remove the chicken from bowl and discard the remaining marinade.

6. Place the chicken breasts onto the grill and cover with the lid.

7. Cook for about 5–7 minutes per side or until desired doneness.

8. Serve hot.

Preparation time: 15 minutes

Cooking time: 14 minutes

Total time: 29 minutes

Servings: 4

Nutritional Values

➢ *Calories 258*

➢ *Net Carbs 0.3 g*

➢ *Total Fat 11.3 g*

➢ *Saturated Fat 1 g*

➢ *Cholesterol 109 mg*

➢ *Sodium 88 mg*

➢ *Total Carbs 0.4 g*

➢ *Fiber 0.1 g*

➢ *Sugar 0.1 g*

➢ *Protein 36.1 g*

Glazed Chicken Thighs

Ingredients

- ½ cup balsamic vinegar
- 1/3 cup low-sodium soy sauce
- 3 tablespoons Yacon syrup
- 4 tablespoons olive oil
- 3 tablespoons chili sauce
- 2 tablespoons garlic, minced
- Salt and ground black pepper, as required
- 8 (6-ounce) grass-fed skinless chicken thighs

How to Prepare

1. In a bowl, add all ingredients (except chicken thighs and sesame seeds) and beat until well combined.

2. In a large plastic zipper bag, add half of marinade and chicken thighs.

3. Seal the bag and shake to coat well.

4. Pace the bag in refrigerator for at least 1 hour, turning bag twice.

5. Reserve remaining marinade in the refrigerator until using.

6. Preheat your oven to 425°F.

7. In a small pan, add reserved marinade over medium heat and bring to a boil.

8. Cook for about 3–5 minutes, stirring occasionally.

9. Remove the pan of sauce from heat and set aside to cool slightly.

10. Remove the chicken from the bag and discard excess marinade.

11. Arrange chicken thighs into a 9x13-inch baking dish in a single layer and coat with some of the cooked marinade.

12. Bake for about 30 minutes, coating with the cooked marinade slightly after every 10 minutes.

13. Serve hot.

Preparation time: 15 minutes

Cooking time: 35 minutes

Total time: 50 minutes

Servings: 8

Nutritional Values

- ➢ *Calories 406*
- ➢ *Net Carbs 4.4 g*
- ➢ *Total Fat 19.6 g*
- ➢ *Saturated Fat 4.5 g*
- ➢ *Cholesterol 151 mg*
- ➢ *Sodium 880 mg*
- ➢ *Total Carbs 4.6 g*
- ➢ *Fiber 0.1 g*
- ➢ *Sugar 2.6 g*
- ➢ *Protein 50 g*

Bacon-Wrapped Chicken Breasts

Ingredients

Chicken Marinade

- ➤ 3 tablespoons balsamic vinegar
- ➤ 3 tablespoons olive oil
- ➤ 2 tablespoons water
- ➤ 1 garlic clove, minced
- ➤ 1 teaspoon dried Italian seasoning
- ➤ ½ teaspoon dried rosemary
- ➤ Salt and ground black pepper, as required

- ➢ 4 (6-ounce) grass-fed skinless, boneless chicken breasts

Stuffing

- ➢ 16 fresh basil leaves
- ➢ 1 large fresh tomato, sliced thinly
- ➢ 4 provolone cheese slices
- ➢ 8 bacon slices
- ➢ ¼ cup Parmesan cheese, grated freshly

How to Prepare

1. For marinade: In a bowl, add all ingredients (except chicken) and mix until well combined.
2. Place 1 chicken breast onto a smooth surface.
3. Hold a sharp knife parallel to work surface, slice the chicken breast horizontally, without cutting all the way through.
4. Repeat with the remaining chicken breasts.
5. Place the breasts in the bowl of marinade and toss to coat well.
6. Refrigerate, covered, for at least 30 minutes.
7. Preheat your oven to 500°F. Grease a baking dish.
8. Remove chicken breast from bowl and arrange onto a smooth surface.

9. Place 4 basil leaves onto the bottom half of a chicken breast. Followed by 2–3 tomato slices and 1 provolone cheese slice.

10. Now, fold the top half over filling.

11. Wrap the breast with 3 bacon slices and secure with toothpicks.

12. Repeat with the remaining chicken breasts and filling.

13. Arrange breasts into the prepared baking dish in a single layer.

14. Bake for about 30 minutes, flipping one halfway through.

15. Remove from the oven and sprinkle each chicken breast with Parmesan cheese evenly.

16. Bake for about 2–3 minutes more.

17. Serve hot.

Preparation time: 15 minutes
Cooking time: 33 minutes
Total time: 48 minutes
Servings: 4

Nutritional Values

➢ *Calories 633*

- *Net Carbs 2.5 g*
- *Total Fat 36 g*
- *Saturated Fat 12.1 g*
- *Cholesterol 207 mg*
- *Sodium 1200 mg*
- *Total Carbs 2.8 g*
- *Fiber 0.3 g*
- *Sugar 0.7 g*
- *Protein 70.6 g*

Chicken Parmigiana

Ingredients

- ➤ 5 (6-ounce) grass-fed skinless, boneless chicken breasts
- ➤ 1 large organic egg, beaten
- ➤ ½ cup superfine blanched almond flour
- ➤ ¼ cup Parmesan cheese, grated
- ➤ ½ teaspoon dried parsley
- ➤ ½ teaspoon paprika
- ➤ ½ teaspoon garlic powder
- ➤ Salt and ground black pepper, as required
- ➤ ¼ cup olive oil
- ➤ 1 cups sugar-free tomato sauce

- ➢ 5 ounces mozzarella cheese, thinly sliced
- ➢ 2 tablespoons fresh parsley, chopped

How to Prepare

1. Preheat your oven to 375°F.
2. Arrange 1 chicken breast between 2 pieces of parchment paper.
3. With a meat mallet, pound the chicken breast into ½-inch thickness
4. Repeat with the remaining chicken breasts.
5. Add the beaten egg into a shallow dish.
6. Place the almond flour, Parmesan, parsley, spices, salt, and black pepper in another shallow dish, and mix well.
7. Dip chicken breasts into the whipped egg and then coat with the flour mixture.
8. Heat the oil in a deep wok over medium-high heat and fry the chicken breasts for about 3 minutes per side.
9. With a slotted spoon, transfer the chicken breasts onto a paper towel-lined plate to drain.
10. In the bottom of a casserole dish, place about ½ cup of tomato sauce and spread evenly.
11. Arrange the chicken breasts over marinara sauce in a single layer.

12. Top with the remaining tomato sauce, followed by mozzarella cheese slices.

13. Bake for about 20 minutes or until done completely.

14. Remove from the oven and serve hot with the garnishing of parsley.

Preparation time: 15 minutes

Cooking time: 26 minutes

Total time: 41 minutes

Servings: 5

Nutritional Values

- *Calories 458*
- *Net Carbs 5.4 g*
- *Total Fat 25.4 g*
- *Saturated Fat 5.4 g*
- *Cholesterol 164 mg*
- *Sodium 722 mg*
- *Total Carbs 7.9 g*
- *Fiber 2.5 g*
- *Sugar 3.7 g*
- *Protein 50.4 g*

Roasted Turkey

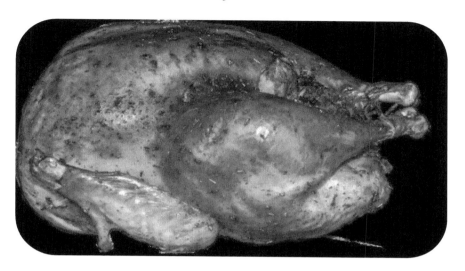

Ingredients

Marinade

- ➤ 1 (2-inch) piece fresh ginger, grated finely
- ➤ 3 large garlic cloves, crushed
- ➤ 1 green chili, chopped finely
- ➤ 1 teaspoon fresh lemon zest, grated finely
- ➤ 5 ounces plain Greek yogurt
- ➤ 3 tablespoons homemade tomato puree
- ➤ 2 tablespoons fresh lemon juice
- ➤ 1½ tablespoons garam masala
- ➤ 1 tablespoon ground cumin
- ➤ 2 teaspoons ground turmeric

Turkey

- ➤ 1 (9-pound) whole turkey, giblets and neck removed
- ➤ Salt and ground black pepper, as required
- ➤ 1 garlic clove, halved
- ➤ 1 lime, halved
- ➤ 1 lemon, halved

How to Prepare

1. For marinade: In a bowl, mix together all ingredients.

2. With a fork, pierce the turkey completely.

3. In a large baking dish, place the turkey and rub with the marinade mixture evenly.

4. Refrigerate to marinate overnight.

5. Remove the turkey from refrigerator and set aside for about 30 minutes before cooking.

6. Preheat your oven to 390°F.

7. Sprinkle turkey with salt and black pepper evenly and stuff the cavity with garlic, lime, and lemon.

8. Arrange the turkey in a large roasting pan and roast for about 30 minutes.

9. Now, reduce the temperature of oven to 350°F.

10. Roast for about 3 hours. (If skin becomes brown during roasting, then cover with a piece of foil.)

11. Remove from the oven and palace the turkey onto a platter for about 15–20 minutes before carving.

12. With a sharp knife, cut the turkey into desired sized pieces and serve.

Preparation time: 15 minutes
Cooking time: 3 hours 30 minutes
Total time: 3¾ hours
Servings: 12

Nutritional Values

- *Calories 595*
- *Net Carbs 2 g*
- *Total Fat 17.3 g*
- *Saturated Fat 5.8 g*
- *Cholesterol 258 mg*
- *Sodium 262 mg*
- *Total Carbs 2.3 g*
- *Fiber 0.3 g*
- *Sugar 1.2 g*
- *Protein 100.3 g*

Roasted Turkey Breast

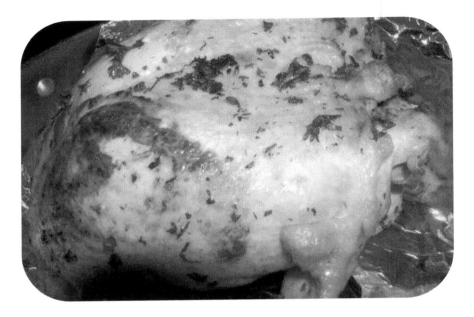

Ingredients

➢ 1 teaspoon onion powder

➢ ½ teaspoon garlic powder

➢ Salt and ground black pepper, as required

➢ 1 (7-pound) bone-in turkey breast

➢ 1½ cups Italian dressing

How to Prepare

1. Preheat your oven to 325°F.

2. Grease a 13x9-inch baking dish.

3. In a bowl, add the onion powder, garlic powder, salt, and black pepper, and mix well.

134

4. Rub the turkey breast with the seasoning mixture generously.

5. Arrange the turkey breast into the prepared baking dish and top with the Italian dressing evenly.

6. Bake for about 2–2½ hours, coating with pan juices occasionally.

7. Remove from the oven and palace the turkey breast onto a platter for about 10–15 minutes before slicing.

8. With a sharp knife, cut the turkey breast into desired-sized slices and serve.

Preparation time: 15 minutes
Cooking time: 2½ hours
Total time: 2¾ hours
Servings: 14

Nutritional Values
  - *Calories 459*
  - *Net Carbs 2.8 g*
  - *Total Fat 23.3 g*
  - *Saturated Fat 5.2 g*
  - *Cholesterol 159 mg*
  - *Sodium 303 mg*
  - *Total Carbs 2.8 g*
  - *Fiber 0 g*
  - *Sugar 2.2 g*
  - *Protein 48.7 g*

Turkey Meatloaf

Ingredients

- ➢ 2 pounds lean ground pork
- ➢ ½ cup yellow onion, chopped
- ➢ ½ cup green bell pepper, seeded and chopped
- ➢ 2 garlic cloves, minced
- ➢ 1 cup cheddar cheese, grated
- ➢ ¼ cup sugar-free ketchup
- ➢ ¼ cup sugar-free HP steak sauce
- ➢ 2 organic eggs, beaten
- ➢ 1 teaspoon dried thyme, crushed
- ➢ Salt and ground black pepper, as required
- ➢ 3 cups fresh spinach, chopped

> 2 cups mozzarella cheese, grated freshly

How to Prepare

1. Preheat your oven to 350°F.

2. Lightly grease a baking dish.

3. In a large bowl, add all the ingredients (except spinach and mozzarella cheese) and mix until well combined.

4. Place a large wax paper onto a smooth surface.

5. Place the meat mixture over wax paper.

6. Add the spinach over meat mixture, pressing slightly.

7. Top with the mozzarella cheese.

8. Roll the wax paper around meat mixture to form a meatloaf.

9. Carefully, remove the wax paper and place meatloaf onto the prepared baking dish.

10. Bake for about 1-1¼ hours.

11. Remove baking dish from the oven and set aside for about 10 minutes before serving.

12. With a sharp knife, cut into desired size slices and serve.

Preparation time: 15 minutes

Cooking time: 1¼ hours

Total time: 1½ hours

Servings: 8

Nutritional Values

- ➢ Calories 280
- ➢ Net Carbs 5.5 g
- ➢ Total Fat 11.1 g
- ➢ Saturated Fat 5.4 g
- ➢ Cholesterol 142 mg
- ➢ Sodium 400 mg
- ➢ Total Carbs 6.2 g
- ➢ Fiber 0.7 g
- ➢ Sugar 3.8 g
- ➢ Protein 37.4 g

MEAT RECIPES

Rosemary Beef Tenderloin

Ingredients

- ➤ 1 (3-pound) grass-fed center-cut beef tenderloin roast
- ➤ 4 garlic cloves, minced
- ➤ 1 tablespoon fresh rosemary, minced and divided
- ➤ Salt and ground black pepper, as required
- ➤ 2 tablespoons olive oil

How to Prepare

1. Preheat your oven to 425°F.
2. Grease a large shallow roasting pan.

3. Place beef into the prepared roasting pan.

4. Rub the beef with garlic, rosemary, salt, and black pepper and drizzle with oil.

5. Roast the beef for about 45–50 minutes.

6. Remove from oven and place the roast onto a cutting board for about 10 minutes.

7. With a sharp knife, cut beef tenderloin into desired-sized slices and serve.

Preparation time: 10 minutes

Cooking time: 50 minutes

Total time: 1 hour

Servings: 10

Nutritional Values

➢ *Calories 314*

➢ *Net Carbs 0.4 g*

➢ *Total Fat 16.9 g*

➢ *Saturated Fat 5.7 g*

➢ *Cholesterol 113 mg*

➢ *Sodium 99 mg*

➢ *Total Carbs 0.6 g*

➢ *Fiber 0.2 g*

➢ *Sugar 0 g*

➢ *Protein 37.8 g*

Garlicky Prime Rib Roast

Ingredients

- ➢ 10 garlic cloves, minced
- ➢ 2 teaspoons dried thyme, crushed
- ➢ 2 tablespoons olive oil
- ➢ Salt and ground black pepper, as required
- ➢ 1 (10-pound) grass-fed prime rib roast

How to Prepare

1. In a bowl, add the garlic, thyme, oil, salt, and black pepper, and mix until well combined.
2. Coat the rib roast evenly with garlic mixture and arrange in a large roasting pan, fatty side up.

3. Set aside to marinate at the room temperature for at least 1 hour.

4. Preheat your oven to 500°F.

5. Place the roasting pan into oven and roast for about 20 minutes.

6. Now, reduce the temperature to 325°F and roast for about 65–75 minutes.

7. Remove from the oven and place the rib roast onto a cutting board for about 10–15 minutes before slicing.

8. With a sharp knife, cut the rib roast into desired-sized slices and serve.

Preparation time: 15 minutes
Cooking time: 1 hour 25 minutes
Total time: 1 hour 40 minutes
Servings: 15

Nutritional Values
➢ *Calories 499*
➢ *Net Carbs 0.6 g*
➢ *Total Fat 25.9 g*
➢ *Saturated Fat 9.6 g*
➢ *Cholesterol 173 mg*
➢ *Sodium 199 mg*
➢ *Total Carbs 0.7 g*
➢ *Fiber 0.1 g*
➢ *Sugar 0 g*
➢ *Protein 61.5 g*

Beef Wellington

Ingredients

- ➢ 2 (4-ounce) grass-fed beef tenderloin steaks, halved
- ➢ Salt and ground black pepper, as required
- ➢ 1 tablespoon butter
- ➢ 1 cup mozzarella cheese, shredded
- ➢ ½ cup almond flour
- ➢ 4 tablespoons liver pate

How to Prepare

1. Preheat your oven to 400°F.
2. Grease a baking sheet.

3. Season the steaks with salt and black pepper evenly.

4. In a frying pan, melt the butter over medium-high heat and sear the beef steaks for about 2–3 minutes per side.

5. Remove frying pan from the heat and set aside to cool completely.

6. In a microwave-safe bowl, add the mozzarella cheese and microwave for about 1 minute.

7. Remove from the microwave and immediately, stir in the almond flour until a dough forms.

8. Place the dough between 2 parchment paper pieces and with a rolling pin, roll to flatten it.

9. Remove the upper parchment paper piece.

10. Divide the rolled dough into 4 pieces.

11. Place 1 tablespoon of pate onto each dough piece and top with 1 steak piece.

12. Cover each steak piece with dough completely.

13. Arrange the covered steak pieces onto the prepared baking sheet in a single layer.

14. Bake for about 20–30 minutes or until the pastry is a golden-brown.

15. Serve warm.

Preparation time: 20 minutes

Cooking time: 40 minutes

Total time: 1 hour

Servings: 4

Nutritional Values

- ➢ *Calories 545*
- ➢ *Net Carbs 3.9 g*
- ➢ *Total Fat 36.6 g*
- ➢ *Saturated Fat 11.3 g*
- ➢ *Cholesterol 190 mg*
- ➢ *Sodium 459 mg*
- ➢ *Total Carbs 6.9 g*
- ➢ *Fiber 3 g*
- ➢ *Sugar 1 g*
- ➢ *Protein 48.2 g*

Beef with Mushroom Sauce

Ingredients

Mushroom Sauce

- ➢ 2 tablespoons butter
- ➢ 3 garlic cloves, minced
- ➢ 1 teaspoon dried thyme
- ➢ 1½ cups fresh button mushrooms, sliced
- ➢ Salt and ground black pepper, as required
- ➢ 7 ounces cream cheese, softened
- ➢ ½ cup heavy cream

Steak
- ➢ 4 (6-ounces) grass-fed beef tenderloin filets

> ➤ Salt and ground black pepper, as required
> ➤ 2 tablespoons butter

How to Prepare

1. For mushroom sauce: In a wok, melt butter over medium heat and sauté the garlic and thyme for about 1 minute.

2. Stir in the mushrooms, salt, and black pepper, and cook for about 5–7 minutes, stirring frequently.

3. Now, adjust the heat to low and stir in cream cheese until smooth.

4. Stir in cream and cook for about 2–3 minutes or until heated completely.

5. Meanwhile, rub the beef filets evenly with salt and black pepper.

6. In a large cast-iron wok, melt the butter over medium heat and cook the filets for about 5–7 minutes per side.

7. Remove the wok of mushroom gravy from heat and stir in the bacon.

8. Place the filets onto serving plates and serve with the topping of mushroom gravy.

Preparation time: 15 minutes
Cooking time: 28 minutes

Total time: 43 minutes

Servings: 4

Nutritional Values

- ➢ *Calories 687*
- ➢ *Net Carbs 3.1 g*
- ➢ *Total Fat 60 g*
- ➢ *Saturated Fat 27.6 g*
- ➢ *Cholesterol 262 mg*
- ➢ *Sodium 375 mg*
- ➢ *Total Carbs 3.5 g*
- ➢ *Fiber 0.4 g*
- ➢ *Sugar 0.6 g*
- ➢ *Protein 54.4 g*

Herbed Rack of Lamb

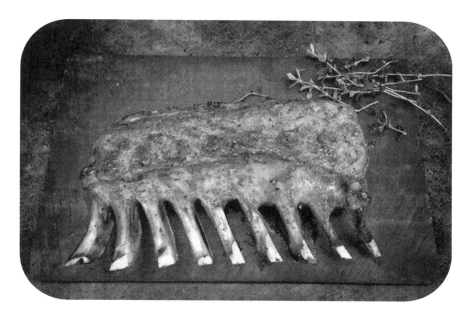

Ingredients

- ➤ 2 (2½-pounds) grass-fed racks of lamb, chine bones removed and trimmed
- ➤ Salt and ground black pepper, as required
- ➤ 2 tablespoons Dijon mustard
- ➤ 2 teaspoons fresh rosemary, chopped
- ➤ 2 teaspoons fresh parsley, chopped
- ➤ 2 teaspoons fresh thyme, chopped

How to Prepare

1. Preheat the charcoal grill to high heat. Grease the grill grate.

2. Season the rack of lamb evenly with salt and black pepper.

3. Coat the meaty sides of racks with mustard, followed by fresh herbs, pressing gently.

4. Carefully, push the coals to one side of the grill.

5. Place racks of lamb over the coals, meaty side down and cook for about 6 minutes.

6. Now, flip the racks and cook for about 3 more minutes.

7. Again, flip the racks down and move to the cooler side of the grill.

8. Cover the grill and cook for about 20 minutes.

9. Remove from the grill and place racks of lamb onto a cutting board for about 10 minutes.

10. With a sharp knife, carve the racks of lamb into chops and serve.

Preparation time: 15 minutes

Cooking time: 29 minutes

Total time: 44 minutes

Servings: 8

Nutritional Values

- ➢ *Calories 532*
- ➢ *Net Carbs 0.2 g*
- ➢ *Total Fat 21 g*
- ➢ *Saturated Fat 7.5 g*
- ➢ *Cholesterol 255 mg*
- ➢ *Sodium 280 mg*
- ➢ *Total Carbs 0.6 g*
- ➢ *Fiber 0.4 g*
- ➢ *Sugar 0 g*
- ➢ *Protein 79.8 g*

Roasted Leg of Lamb

Ingredients

- ➤ 1/3 cup fresh parsley, minced
- ➤ 4 garlic cloves, minced
- ➤ 1 teaspoon fresh lemon zest, finely grated
- ➤ 1 tablespoon ground coriander
- ➤ 1 tablespoon ground cumin
- ➤ 1 tablespoon smoked paprika
- ➤ 1 tablespoon red pepper flakes, finely crushed
- ➤ ½ teaspoon ground allspice
- ➤ 1/3 cup olive oil
- ➤ 1 (5-pound) grass-fed bone-in leg of lamb, trimmed

How to Prepare

1. In a large bowl, place all ingredients (except the leg of lamb) and mix well.

2. Coat the leg of lamb with marinade mixture generously.

3. With a plastic wrap, cover the leg of lamb and refrigerate to marinate for about 6–8 hours.

4. Remove from refrigerator and keep in room temperature for about 30 minutes before roasting.

5. Preheat your oven to 350°F. Arrange the oven rack in the center of oven.

6. Arrange a lightly, greased rack in the roasting pan.

7. Place the leg of lamb over rack into the roasting pan.

8. Roast for about 1¼-1½ hours, rotating the pan once halfway through.

9. Remove from oven and place the leg of lamb onto a cutting board for about 10–15 minutes.

10. With a sharp knife, cut the leg of lamb into desired size slices and serve.

Preparation time: 15 minutes
Cooking time: 1½ hours
Total time: 1¾ hours
Servings: 8

Nutritional Values

- ➢ Calories 610
- ➢ Net Carbs 1.3 g
- ➢ Total Fat 29.6 g
- ➢ Saturated Fat 8.7 g
- ➢ Cholesterol 255 mg
- ➢ Sodium 219 mg
- ➢ Total Carbs 2 g
- ➢ Fiber 0.7 g
- ➢ Sugar 0.2 g
- ➢ Protein 80.1 g

Stuffed Pork Tenderloin

Ingredients

- ➢ 1 pound pork tenderloin
- ➢ 1 tablespoon unsalted butter
- ➢ 2 teaspoons garlic, minced
- ➢ 2 ounces fresh spinach
- ➢ 4 ounces cream cheese, softened
- ➢ 1 teaspoon liquid smoke
- ➢ Salt and ground black pepper, as required

How to Prepare

1. Preheat your oven to 350°F.

2. Line a casserole dish with a piece of foil.

3. Arrange the pork tenderloin between 2 plastic wraps and with a meat tenderizer, pound until flat.

4. Carefully, cut the edges of tenderloin to shape into a rectangle.

5. Melt the butter in a large wok over medium heat and sauté the garlic for about 1 minute.

6. Add the spinach, cream cheese, liquid smoke, salt, and black pepper, and cook for about 3–4 minutes.

7. Remove the wok from heat and let it cool slightly.

8. Place the spinach mixture onto pork tenderloin about ½-inch from the edges.

9. Carefully, roll tenderloin into a log and secure with toothpicks.

10. Arrange tenderloin into the prepared casserole dish, seam-side down.

11. Bake for about 1¼ hours.

12. Remove the casserole dish from oven and let it cool slightly before cutting.

13. Cut the tenderloin into desired size slices and serve.

Preparation time: 20 minutes

Cooking time: 1 hour 20 minutes

Total time: 1 hour 40 minutes

Servings: 3

Nutritional Values

- ➢ *Calories 389*
- ➢ *Net Carbs 1.8 g*
- ➢ *Total Fat 22.4 g*
- ➢ *Saturated Fat 12.6 g*
- ➢ *Cholesterol 162 mg*
- ➢ *Sodium 291 mg*
- ➢ *Total Carbs 2.3 g*
- ➢ *Fiber 0.5 g*
- ➢ *Sugar 0.2 g*
- ➢ *Protein 43.1 g*

Sticky Pork Ribs

Ingredients

- ¼ cups granulated erythritol
- 1 tablespoon garlic powder
- 1 tablespoon paprika
- ½ teaspoon red chili powder
- 4 pounds pork ribs, membrane removed
- Salt and ground black pepper, as required
- 1½ teaspoons liquid smoke
- 1½ cups sugar-free BBQ sauce

How to Prepare

1. Preheat your oven to 300°F. Line a large baking sheet with 2 layers of foil, shiny-side out.

2. In a bowl, mix well erythritol, garlic powder, paprika, and chili powder.

3. Season the ribs with salt and black pepper and then coat with the liquid smoke.

4. Now, rub the ribs evenly with erythritol mixture.

5. Arrange ribs onto the prepared baking sheet, meaty side down.

6. Arrange 2 layers of foil on top of ribs and then, roll and crimp edges tightly.

7. Bake for about 2–2½ hours or until desired doneness.

8. Remove the baking sheet from oven and place the ribs onto a cutting board.

9. Now, set the oven to broiler.

10. With a sharp knife, cut the ribs into serving sized portions and evenly coat with the barbecue sauce.

11. Arrange the ribs onto a broiler pan, bony side up.

12. Broil for about 1–2 minutes per side.

13. Remove from the oven and serve hot.

Preparation time: 15 minutes
Cooking time: 2 hours 34 minutes

Total time: 2 hours 49 minutes

Servings: 8

Nutritional Values

> ➤ *Calories 634*
> ➤ *Net Carbs 0 g*
> ➤ *Total Fat 40.5 g*
> ➤ *Saturated Fat 14.3 g*
> ➤ *Cholesterol 234 mg*
> ➤ *Sodium 265 mg*
> ➤ *Total Carbs 3.4 g*
> ➤ *Fiber 0.5 g*
> ➤ *Sugar 1.3 g*
> ➤ *Protein 60.4 g*

SEAFOOD & FISH RECIPES

Grilled Salmon

Ingredients

- ➢ 2 garlic cloves, minced
- ➢ 1 tablespoon fresh lemon zest, grated
- ➢ 2 tablespoons butter, melted
- ➢ 2 tablespoons fresh lemon juice
- ➢ Salt and ground black pepper, as required
- ➢ 4 (6-ounce) skinless, boneless salmon fillets

How to Prepare

1. Preheat the grill to medium-high heat. Grease the grill grate.
2. In a large bowl, mix together all ingredients except salmon fillets.
3. Add the salmon fillets and coat with garlic mixture generously.
4. Place the salmon steaks onto the grill and cook for about 6–7 minutes per side.
5. Serve hot.

Preparation time: 15 minutes
Cooking time: 14 minutes
Total time: 29 minutes
Servings: 4

Nutritional Values

- ➢ *Calories 281*
- ➢ *Net Carbs 0.8 g*
- ➢ *Total Fat 16.3 g*
- ➢ *Saturated Fat 5.2 g*
- ➢ *Cholesterol 90 mg*
- ➢ *Sodium 157 mg*
- ➢ *Total Carbs 1 g*
- ➢ *Fiber 0.2 g*
- ➢ *Sugar 0.3 g*
- ➢ *Protein 33.3 g*

Salmon with Dill

Ingredients

- ¼ cup fresh dill, chopped and divided
- 1 teaspoon fresh lemon zest
- ½ teaspoon smoked paprika
- ½ teaspoon fennel seeds, crushed lightly
- Salt and ground black pepper, as required
- 2 (6-ounce) skinless, boneless salmon fillets
- 1 tablespoon fresh lemon juice
- 2 tablespoons olive oil

How to Prepare

1. In a bowl, place 2 tablespoons of dill, lemon zest, paprika, fennel seeds, salt, and black pepper, and mix well.

2. Season the salmon fillet with dill mixture evenly and then drizzle with lemon juice.

3. Drizzle each salmon fillet with lemon juice.

4. In a large wok, heat oil over medium heat.

5. In the wok, place the salmon fillets in a single layer.

6. Reduce the heat to the low and cook for about 20 minutes.

7. Flip and cook for about 5 minutes more.

8. With a slotted spoon, transfer the salmon fillets onto a paper towel-lined plate to drain.

9. Serve immediately with the topping of remaining dill.

Preparation time: 15 minutes

Cooking time: 25 minutes

Total time: 40 minutes

Servings: 2

Nutritional Values

➢ *Calories 351*

- *Net Carbs 0.4 g*
- *Total Fat 24.7 g*
- *Saturated Fat 3.6 g*
- *Cholesterol 75 mg*
- *Sodium 155 mg*
- *Total Carbs 0.9 g*
- *Fiber 0.5 g*
- *Sugar 0.3 g*
- *Protein 33.2 g*

Lemony Trout

Ingredients

- ➤ 2 (1½-pound) wild-caught trout, gutted and cleaned
- ➤ Salt and ground black pepper, as required
- ➤ 1 lemon, sliced
- ➤ 2 tablespoons fresh dill, minced
- ➤ 2 tablespoons butter, melted
- ➤ 2 tablespoons fresh lemon juice

How to Prepare

1. Preheat your oven to 475°F.

2. Arrange a wire rack onto a foil-lined baking sheet.

3. Sprinkle the trout with salt and black pepper from inside and outside generously.

4. Fill the cavity of each fish with lemon slices and dill.

5. Place the trout onto prepared baking sheet and drizzle with the melted butter and lemon juice.

6. Bake for about 25 minutes.

7. Remove the baking sheet from oven and transfer the trout onto a serving platter.

8. Serve hot.

Preparation time: 15 minutes

Cooking time: 25 minutes

Total time: 40 minutes

Servings: 6

Nutritional Values

➢ *Calories 469*

➢ *Net Carbs 0.7 g*

➢ *Total Fat 23.1 g*

➢ *Saturated Fat 5.8 g*

➢ *Cholesterol 178 mg*

➢ *Sodium 210 mg*

➢ *Total Carbs 0.9 g*

➢ *Fiber 0.2 g*

➢ *Sugar 0.2 g*

➢ *Protein 60.7 g*

Grouper Curry

Ingredients

- ➢ 1 tablespoon coconut oil
- ➢ 1 small yellow onion, chopped
- ➢ 2 garlic cloves, minced
- ➢ 1 teaspoon fresh ginger, minced
- ➢ 1 large tomato, peeled and chopped
- ➢ 1 tablespoons curry powder
- ➢ ¼ cup water
- ➢ 1¼ cups unsweetened coconut milk
- ➢ 1½ pounds skinless grouper fillets, cubed into 2-inch size
- ➢ Salt, as required
- ➢ 2 tablespoons fresh parsley, chopped

Instructions

1. In a large wok, melt the coconut oil over medium heat and sauté the onion, garlic and ginger for about 5 minutes.

2. Add the tomatoes and curry powder and cook for about 2–3 minutes, crushing with the back of spoon.

3. Add the water and coconut milk and bring to a gentle boil.

4. Stir in grouper pieces and cook for about 4–5 minutes.

5. Stir in the salt and basil leaves and serve hot.

Preparation time: 15 minutes
Cooking time: 15 minutes
Total time: 30 minutes
Servings: 6

Nutritional Values

➢ *Calories 245*
➢ *Net Carbs 3.7 g*
➢ *Total Fat 10.9 g*
➢ *Saturated Fat 8.6 g*
➢ *Cholesterol 53 mg*
➢ *Sodium 107 mg*
➢ *Total Carbs 4.8 g*
➢ *Fiber 1.1 g*
➢ *Sugar 2.6 g*
➢ *Protein 29.5 g*

Tuna Casserole

Ingredients

- ➤ 2 ounces butter
- ➤ 5 1/3 ounces celery stalks, chopped
- ➤ 1 yellow onion, chopped
- ➤ 1 green bell pepper, seeded and chopped
- ➤ 16 ounces canned tuna in olive oil, drained
- ➤ 4 ounces Parmesan cheese, shredded
- ➤ 1 cup mayonnaise
- ➤ 1 teaspoon chili flakes
- ➤ Salt and ground black pepper, as required

How to Prepare

1. Preheat your oven to 400°F.

2. Grease a large baking dish.

3. Melt the butter in a large frying pan and sauté the celery, onion and bell pepper or about 4–5 minutes.

4. Now, add in the salt and black pepper and remove the pan from heat.

5. Place the tuna, Parmesan cheese, mayonnaise, and chili flakes into the prepared baking dish and mix well.

6. Add the onion mixture and gently, stir to combine.

7. Bake for about 15–20 minutes or until the top becomes golden brown.

8. Remove the baking dish from oven and let it cool for about 5 minutes before serving.

Preparation time: 15 minutes

Cooking time: 25 minutes

Total time: 40 minutes

Servings: 5

Nutritional Values

➢ *Calories 629*

➢ *Net Carbs 3.5 g*

- *Total Fat 53.5 g*
- *Saturated Fat 15.4 g*
- *Cholesterol 85 mg*
- *Sodium 666 mg*
- *Total Carbs 4.9 g*
- *Fiber 1.4 g*
- *Sugar 1.9 g*
- *Protein 32.1 g*

Shrimp with Asparagus

Ingredients

- ➢ 2 tablespoons butter
- ➢ 1 pound asparagus, trimmed
- ➢ 1 pound shrimp, peeled and deveined
- ➢ 4 garlic cloves, minced
- ➢ 2 tablespoons fresh lemon juice
- ➢ 1/3 cup homemade chicken broth

How to Prepare

1. Melt butter in a large wok over medium-high heat.

2. Add all the ingredients except broth and cook for about 2 minutes, without stirring.

3. Stir the mixture and cook for about 3–4 minutes, stirring occasionally.

4. Stir in the broth and cook for about 2–4 more minutes.

5. Serve hot.

Preparation time: 15 minutes
Cooking time: 10 minutes
Total time: 25 minutes
Servings: 4

Nutritional Values

> *Calories 217*
> *Net Carbs 4.8 g*
> *Total Fat 8 g*
> *Saturated Fat 4.3 g*
> *Cholesterol 254 mg*
> *Sodium 384 mg*
> *Total Carbs 36.2 g*
> *Fiber 7.2 g*
> *Sugar 2.2 g*
> *Protein 29 g*

Shrimp Curry

Ingredients

- ➢ 2 tablespoons coconut oil
- ➢ ½ of yellow onion, minced
- ➢ 2 garlic cloves, minced
- ➢ 1 teaspoon ground turmeric
- ➢ 1 teaspoon ground cumin
- ➢ 1 teaspoon paprika
- ➢ 1 (14-ounce) can unsweetened coconut milk
- ➢ 1 large tomato, chopped finely
- ➢ Salt, as required

- ➢ 1 pound shrimp, peeled and deveined
- ➢ 2 tablespoons fresh cilantro, chopped

How to Prepare

1. Melt coconut oil in a large wok over medium heat and sauté the onion for about 5 minutes.
2. Add the garlic, and spices and sauté for about 1 minute.
3. Add the coconut milk, tomato, and salt, and bring to a gentle boil.
4. Lower the heat to low and simmer for about 10 minutes, stirring occasionally.
5. Stir in the shrimp and cilantro and simmer for about 4–5 minutes.
6. Remove the wok from heat and serve hot.

Preparation time: 15 minutes

Cooking time: 21 minutes

Total time: 36 minutes

Servings: 4

Nutritional Values

- ➢ *Calories 359*

- ➢ *Net Carbs 6 g*
- ➢ *Total Fat 22.7 g*
- ➢ *Saturated Fat 18.9 g*
- ➢ *Cholesterol 239 mg*
- ➢ *Sodium 353 mg*
- ➢ *Total Carbs 7 g*
- ➢ *Fiber 1 g*
- ➢ *Sugar 3.6 g*
- ➢ *Protein 27.7 g*

Seafood Stew

Ingredients

- ➤ 2 tablespoons butter
- ➤ 1 medium yellow onion, chopped
- ➤ 2 garlic cloves, minced
- ➤ 1 Serrano pepper, chopped
- ➤ ¼ teaspoon red pepper flakes, crushed
- ➤ ½ pound fresh tomatoes, chopped
- ➤ 1½ cups homemade fish broth
- ➤ 1 pound red snapper fillets, cubed
- ➤ ½ pound shrimp, peeled and deveined
- ➤ ¼ pound fresh squid, cleaned and cut into rings

- ¼ pound bay scallops
- ¼ pound mussels
- 2 tablespoons fresh lime juice
- ½ cup fresh basil, chopped

How to Prepare

1. In a large soup pan, melt butter over medium heat and sauté the onion for about 5–6 minutes.
2. Add the garlic, Serrano pepper, and red pepper flakes, and sauté for about 1 minute.
3. Add tomatoes and broth and bring to a gentle simmer.
4. Reduce the heat and cook for about 10 minutes.
5. Add the tilapia and cook for about 2 minutes.
6. Stir in the remaining seafood and cook for about 6–8 minutes.
7. Stir in the lemon juice, basil, salt, and black pepper, and remove from heat.
8. Serve hot.

Preparation time: 20 minutes
Cooking time: 30 minutes
Total time: 50 minutes
Servings: 8

Nutritional Values

- Calories 190
- Net Carbs 3.8 g
- Total Fat 5.4 g
- Saturated Fat 2.4 g
- Cholesterol 136 mg
- Sodium 262 mg
- Total Carbs 4.5 g
- Fiber 0.7 g
- Sugar 1.4 g
- Protein 29.2 g

SALAD RECIPES

Tomato & Mozzarella Salad

Ingredients

- ➤ 4 cups cherry tomatoes, halved
- ➤ 1½ pounds mozzarella cheese, cubed
- ➤ ¼ cup fresh basil leaves, chopped
- ➤ ¼ cup olive oil
- ➤ 2 tablespoons fresh lemon juice
- ➤ 1 teaspoon fresh oregano, minced
- ➤ 1 teaspoon fresh parsley, minced
- ➤ 2–4 drops liquid stevia

> Salt and ground black pepper, as required

How to Prepare

1. In a salad bowl, mix together tomatoes, mozzarella, and basil.
2. In a small bowl, add remaining ingredients and beat until well combined.
3. Place dressing over salad and toss to coat well.
4. Serve immediately.

Preparation time: 15 minutes
Total time: 15 minutes
Servings: 8

Nutritional Values

> *Calories 87*
> *Net Carbs 2.7 g*
> *Total Fat 7.5 g*
> *Saturated Fat 1.5 g*
> *Cholesterol 3 mg*
> *Sodium 57 mg*
> *Total Carbs 3.9 g*
> *Fiber 1.2 g*
> *Sugar 2.5 g*
> *Protein 2.4 g*

Cucumber & Tomato Salad

Ingredients

Salad

- ➤ 3 large English cucumbers, thinly sliced
- ➤ 2 cups tomatoes, chopped
- ➤ 6 cups lettuce, torn

Dressing

- ➤ 4 tablespoons olive oil
- ➤ 2 tablespoons balsamic vinegar
- ➤ 1 tablespoon fresh lemon juice
- ➤ Salt and ground black pepper, as required

How to Prepare

1. For salad: In a large bowl, add the cucumbers, onion, cucumbers, and mix.
2. For dressing: In a small bowl, add all the ingredients and beat until well combined.
3. Place the dressing over the salad and toss to coat well.
4. Serve immediately.

Preparation time: 15 minutes
Total time: 15 minutes
Servings: 8

Nutritional Values

- ➢ *Calories 86*
- ➢ *Net Carbs 0 g*
- ➢ *Total Fat 7.3 g*
- ➢ *Saturated Fat 1 g*
- ➢ *Cholesterol 0 mg*
- ➢ *Sodium 27 mg*
- ➢ *Total Carbs 5.1 g*
- ➢ *Fiber 1.4 g*
- ➢ *Sugar 2.8 g*
- ➢ *Protein 1.1 g*

Chicken & Strawberry Salad

Ingredients

- ➢ 2 pounds grass-fed boneless skinless chicken breasts
- ➢ ½ cup olive oil
- ➢ ¼ cup fresh lemon juice
- ➢ 2 tablespoons granulated erythritol
- ➢ 1 garlic clove, minced
- ➢ Salt and ground black pepper, as required
- ➢ 4 cups fresh strawberries
- ➢ 8 cups fresh spinach, torn

How to Prepare

1. For marinade: in a large bowl, add oil, lemon juice, erythritol, garlic, salt, and black pepper, and beat until well combined.

2. In a large resealable plastic bag, place the chicken and ¾ cup of marinade.

3. Seal bag and shake to coat well.

4. Refrigerate overnight.

5. Cover the bowl of remaining marinade and refrigerate before serving.

6. Preheat the grill to medium heat. Grease the grill grate.

7. Remove the chicken from bag and discard the marinade.

8. Place the chicken onto grill grate and grill, covered for about 5–8 minutes per side.

9. Remove chicken from grill and cut into bite sized pieces.

10. In a large bowl, add the chicken pieces, strawberries, and spinach, and mix.

11. Place the reserved marinade and toss to coat.

12. Serve immediately.

Preparation time: 20 minutes

Cooking time: 16 minutes

Total time: 36 minutes

Servings: 8

Nutritional Values

- ➢ *Calories 356*
- ➢ *Net Carbs 4 g*
- ➢ *Total Fat 21.4 g*
- ➢ *Saturated Fat 4 g*
- ➢ *Cholesterol 101 mg*
- ➢ *Sodium 143 mg*
- ➢ *Total Carbs 6.1 g*
- ➢ *Fiber 2.1 g*
- ➢ *Sugar 3.8 g*
- ➢ *Protein 34.2 g*

Salmon Salad

Ingredients

- 12 hard-boiled organic eggs, peeled and cubed
- 1 pound smoked salmon
- 3 celery stalks, chopped
- 1 yellow onion, chopped
- 4 tablespoons fresh dill, chopped
- 2 cups mayonnaise
- Salt and ground black pepper, as required
- 8 cups fresh lettuce leaves

How to Prepare

1. In a large serving bowl, add all the ingredients (except the lettuce leaves) and gently stir to combine.
2. Cover and refrigerate to chill before serving.
3. Divide the lettuce onto serving plates and top with the salmon salad.
4. Serve immediately.

Preparation time: 15 minutes
Total time: 15 minutes
Servings: 8

Nutritional Values

- *Calories 539*
- *Net Carbs 3.5 g*
- *Total Fat 49.2 g*
- *Saturated Fat 8.6 g*
- *Cholesterol 279 mg*
- *Sodium 1618 mg*
- *Total Carbs 4.5 g*
- *Fiber 1 g*
- *Sugar 1.7 g*
- *Protein 19.4 g*

Shrimp Salad

Ingredients

- ➢ 1 tablespoon unsalted butter
- ➢ 1 garlic clove, crushed and divided
- ➢ 2 tablespoons fresh rosemary, chopped
- ➢ 1 pound shrimp, peeled and deveined
- ➢ Salt and ground black pepper, as required
- ➢ 4 cups fresh arugula
- ➢ 2 cups lettuce, torn
- ➢ 2 tablespoons olive oil
- ➢ 2 tablespoons fresh lime juice

How to Prepare

1. In a large wok, melt the butter over medium heat and sauté 1 garlic clove for about 1 minute.

2. Add the shrimp with salt and black pepper and cook for about 4–5 minutes.

3. Remove from the heat and set aside to cool.

4. Ina large bowl, add the shrimp, arugula, oil, lime juice, salt, and black pepper, and gently toss to coat.

5. Serve immediately.

Preparation time: 15 minutes
Cooking time: 6 minutes
Total time: 21 minutes
Servings: 6

Nutritional Values

➢ *Calories 157*
➢ *Net Carbs 2.3 g*
➢ *Total Fat 8.2 g*
➢ *Saturated Fat 2.4 g*
➢ *Cholesterol 164 mg*
➢ *Sodium 230 mg*
➢ *Total Carbs 3.1 g*
➢ *Fiber 0.8 g*
➢ *Sugar 0.5 g*
➢ *Protein 17.7 g*

SOUP RECIPES

Chilled Cucumber Soup

Ingredients

- ➢ 1 cup English cucumber, peeled and chopped
- ➢ 1 scallion, chopped
- ➢ 2 tablespoons fresh parsley leaves
- ➢ 2 tablespoons fresh basil leaves
- ➢ ¼ teaspoon fresh lime zest, grated freshly
- ➢ 1 cup unsweetened coconut milk
- ➢ ¼ cup water
- ➢ ½ tablespoon fresh lime juice

> Salt and ground black pepper, as required

How to Prepare

1. Add all the ingredients in a high-speed blender and pulse on high speed until smooth.
2. Transfer the soup into a large serving bowl.
3. Cover the bowl of soup and place in refrigerator to chill for about 6 hours.
4. Serve chilled.

Preparation time: 15 minutes
Total time: 15 minutes
Servings: 2

Nutritional Values

> *Calories 193*
> *Net Carbs 5.1 g*
> *Total Fat 16.6 g*
> *Saturated Fat 15 g*
> *Cholesterol 0 mg*
> *Sodium 120 mg*
> *Total Carbs 5.8 g*
> *Fiber 0.7 g*
> *Sugar 4.1 g*
> *Protein 2.2 g*

Creamy Mushroom Soup

Ingredients

- ➤ 3 tablespoons unsalted butter
- ➤ 1 scallion, sliced
- ➤ 1 large garlic clove, crushed
- ➤ 5 cups fresh button mushrooms, sliced
- ➤ 2 cups homemade vegetable broth
- ➤ Salt and ground black pepper, as required
- ➤ 1 cup heavy cream

How to Prepare

1. In a large soup pan, melt the butter over medium heat and sauté the scallion and garlic for about 2–3 minutes.

2. Add the mushrooms cook fry for about 5–6 minutes, stirring frequently.

3. Stir in the broth and bring to a boil.

4. Cook for about 5 minutes.

5. Remove from the heat and with a stick blender, blend the soup until smooth.

6. Return the pan over medium heat.

7. Stir in the cream, salt and black pepper and cook for about 2–3 minutes, stirring continuously.

8. Remove from the heat and serve hot.

Preparation time: 15 minutes

Cooking time: 20 minutes

Total time: 35 minutes

Servings: 4

Nutritional Values

➢ *Calories 208*

➢ *Net Carbs 4.3 g*

- *Total Fat 20 g*
- *Saturated Fat 12.4 g*
- *Cholesterol 64 mg*
- *Sodium 382 mg*
- *Total Carbs 5.8 g*
- *Fiber 1.5 g*
- *Sugar 2.6 g*
- *Protein 3.6 g*

Broccoli Soup

Ingredients

- ➤ 5 cups homemade chicken broth
- ➤ 20 ounces small broccoli florets
- ➤ 12 ounces cheddar cheese, cubed
- ➤ Salt and ground black pepper, as required
- ➤ 1 cup heavy cream

How to Prepare

1. In a large soup pan, add the broth and broccoli over medium-high heat and bring to a boil.

2. Reduce the heat to low and simmer, covered for about 5–7 minutes.

3. Stir in the cheese and cook for about 2–3 minutes, stirring continuously.

4. Stir in the salt, black pepper, and cream, and cook for about 2 minutes.

5. Serve hot.

Preparation time: 10 minutes
Cooking time: 15 minutes
Total time: 25 minutes
Servings: 6

Nutritional Values

➢ *Calories 362*
➢ *Net Carbs 5.5 g*
➢ *Total Fat 27.6 g*
➢ *Saturated Fat 16.9 g*
➢ *Cholesterol 87 mg*
➢ *Sodium 1000 mg*
➢ *Total Carbs 8 g*
➢ *Fiber 2.5 g*
➢ *Sugar 2.5 g*
➢ *Protein 21.2 g*

Creamy Chicken Soup

Ingredients

- ➢ 1 tablespoon butter
- ➢ 1¼ cups tomatoes, chopped finely
- ➢ 2 Serrano peppers, chopped
- ➢ 1 tablespoon taco seasoning
- ➢ 1 pound grass-fed boneless skinless chicken breasts
- ➢ 3¼ cups homemade chicken broth
- ➢ 8 ounces cream cheese, softened
- ➢ ½ cup heavy cream
- ➢ Salt, as required
- ➢ 2 tablespoons fresh cilantro, chopped

How to Prepare

1. In a Dutch oven, melt butter over medium heat and cook the tomatoes and Serrano for about 1–2 minutes.

2. Add the chicken, and broth and bring to a boil.

3. Now, reduce the heat to medium-low and simmer, covered for about 25 minutes.

4. With a slotted spoon, transfer the chicken breasts onto a plate.

5. With 2 forks, shred the meat.

6. In the pan of soup, add the cream cheese, and cream and cook for about 2–3 minutes, stirring continuously.

7. Remove the soup pan from heat and with an immersion blender, blend the soup until smooth.

8. Return the pan over medium heat and stir in the shredded chicken and salt.

9. Cook for about 1–2 minutes.

10. Serve hot with the topping of cilantro.

Preparation time: 15 minutes

Cooking time: 35 minutes

Total time: 50 minutes

Servings: 4

Nutritional Values

➢ *Calories 533*

- ➤ *Net Carbs 4.3 g*
- ➤ *Total Fat 37.8 g*
- ➤ *Saturated Fat 20.4 g*
- ➤ *Cholesterol 191 mg*
- ➤ *Sodium 954 mg*
- ➤ *Total Carbs 5.1 g*
- ➤ *Fiber 0.8 g*
- ➤ *Sugar 2.3 g*
- ➤ *Protein 41.9 g*

Meatballs Soup

Ingredients

Meatballs

- ➤ 1 pound lean ground turkey
- ➤ 1 garlic clove, minced
- ➤ 1 organic egg, beaten
- ➤ ¼ cup Parmesan cheese, grated
- ➤ Salt and ground black pepper, as required

Soup

- ➤ 1 tablespoon olive oil
- ➤ 1 small yellow onion, finely chopped

- ➢ 1 garlic clove, minced
- ➢ 6 cups homemade chicken broth
- ➢ 7 cups fresh spinach, chopped
- ➢ Salt and ground black pepper, as required

How to Prepare

1. For meatballs: In a bowl, add all ingredients and mix until well combined.
2. Make equal sized small balls from mixture.
3. In a large soup pan, heat oil over medium heat and sauté onion for about 5–6 minutes.
4. Add the garlic and sauté for about 1 minute.
5. Add in the broth and bring to a boil.
6. Carefully, place the balls in pan and bring to a boil.
7. Reduce the heat to low and cook for about 10 minutes.
8. Stir in the kale and bring the soup to a gentle simmer.
9. Simmer for about 2–3 minutes.
10. Season the soup with the salt and black pepper and serve hot.

Preparation time: 20 minutes
Cooking time: 25 minutes
Total time: 45 minutes
Servings: 6

Nutritional Values

- ➢ Calories 203
- ➢ Net Carbs 2.7 g
- ➢ Total Fat 10.8 g
- ➢ Saturated Fat 3.1 g
- ➢ Cholesterol 84 mg
- ➢ Sodium 915 mg
- ➢ Total Carbs 3.7 g
- ➢ Fiber 1 g
- ➢ Sugar 1.4 g
- ➢ Protein 23.1 g

SMOOTHIES RECIPES

Almond Smoothie

Ingredients

- ➤ ¾ cup almonds, chopped
- ➤ ½ cup heavy whipping cream
- ➤ 2 teaspoons butter, melted
- ➤ ¼ teaspoon organic vanilla extract
- ➤ 7–8 drops liquid stevia
- ➤ 1 cup unsweetened almond milk

> ¼ cup ice cubes

How to Prepare

1. In a blender, put all the listed ingredients and pulse until creamy.
2. Pour the smoothie into two glasses and serve immediately.

Preparation time: 10 minutes
Total time: 10 minutes
Servings: 2

Nutritional Values

> *Calories 365*
> *Net Carbs 4.5 g*
> *Total Fat 34.55 g*
> *Saturated Fat 10.8 g*
> *Cholesterol 51 mg*
> *Sodium 129 mg*
> *Total Carbs 9.5 g*
> *Fiber 5 g*
> *Sugar 1.6 g*
> *Protein 8.7 g*

Mocha Smoothie

Ingredients

- ➢ 2 teaspoons instant espresso powder
- ➢ 2–3 tablespoons granulated erythritol
- ➢ 2 teaspoons cacao powder
- ➢ ½ cup plain Greek yogurt
- ➢ 1 cup unsweetened almond milk
- ➢ 1 cup ice cubes

How to Prepare

1. In a blender, put all the listed ingredients and pulse until creamy.

2. Pour the smoothie into two glasses and serve immediately.

Preparation time: 10 minutes
Total time: 10 minutes
Servings: 2

Nutritional Values

- ➤ *Calories 70*
- ➤ *Net Carbs 5.5 g*
- ➤ *Total Fat 2.8 g*
- ➤ *Saturated Fat 1 g*
- ➤ *Cholesterol 4 mg*
- ➤ *Sodium 133 mg*
- ➤ *Total Carbs 6.5 g*
- ➤ *Fiber 1 g*
- ➤ *Sugar 4.3 g*
- ➤ *Protein 4.4 g*

Strawberry Smoothie

Ingredients

- ➤ 4 ounces frozen strawberries
- ➤ 2 teaspoons granulated erythritol
- ➤ ½ teaspoon organic vanilla extract
- ➤ 1/3 cup heavy whipping cream
- ➤ 1¼ cups unsweetened almond milk
- ➤ ½ cup ice cubes

How to Prepare

1. In a blender, put all the listed ingredients and pulse until creamy.

2. Pour the smoothie into two glasses and serve immediately.

Preparation time: 10 minutes
Total time: 10 minutes
Servings: 2

Nutritional Values

> ➢ *Calories 115*
> ➢ *Net Carbs 4.5 g*
> ➢ *Total Fat 9.8 g*
> ➢ *Saturated Fat 4.8 g*
> ➢ *Cholesterol 27 mg*
> ➢ *Sodium 121 mg*
> ➢ *Total Carbs 6.3 g*
> ➢ *Fiber 1.8 g*
> ➢ *Sugar 2.9 g*
> ➢ *Protein 1.4 g*

Raspberry Smoothie

Ingredients

- ➢ ¾ cup fresh raspberries
- ➢ 3 tablespoons heavy whipping cream
- ➢ 1/3 ounce cream cheese
- ➢ 1 cup unsweetened almond milk
- ➢ ½ cup ice, crushed

How to Prepare

1. In a blender, put all the listed ingredients and pulse until creamy.

2. Pour the smoothie into two glasses and serve immediately.

Preparation time: 10 minutes

Total time: 10 minutes

Servings: 2

Nutritional Values

- ➤ *Calories 138*
- ➤ *Net Carbs 3.8 g*
- ➤ *Total Fat 12 g*
- ➤ *Saturated Fat 6.4 g*
- ➤ *Cholesterol 36 mg*
- ➤ *Sodium 115 mg*
- ➤ *Total Carbs 7.3 g*
- ➤ *Fiber 3.5 g*
- ➤ *Sugar 2.1 g*
- ➤ *Protein 1.9 g*

Pumpkin Smoothie

Ingredients

- ➤ ½ cup homemade pumpkin puree
- ➤ 4 ounces cream cheese, softened
- ➤ ¼ cup heavy cream
- ➤ ½ teaspoon pumpkin pie spice
- ➤ ¼ teaspoon ground cinnamon
- ➤ 8 drops liquid stevia
- ➤ 1 teaspoon organic vanilla extract
- ➤ 1 cup unsweetened almond milk
- ➤ ¼ cup ice cubes

How to Prepare

1. In a blender, put all the listed ingredients and pulse until creamy.
2. Pour the smoothie into two glasses and serve immediately.

Preparation time: 10 minutes

Total time: 10 minutes

Servings: 2

Nutritional Values

- ➢ *Calories 296*
- ➢ *Net Carbs 5.4 g*
- ➢ *Total Fat 27.1 g*
- ➢ *Saturated Fat 16.1g*
- ➢ *Cholesterol 83 mg*
- ➢ *Sodium 266 mg*
- ➢ *Total Carbs 8 g*
- ➢ *Fiber 2.6 g*
- ➢ *Sugar 2.4 g*
- ➢ *Protein 5.6 g*

Spinach & Avocado Smoothie

Ingredients

- ➤ ½ large avocado, peeled, pitted, and roughly chopped
- ➤ 2 cups fresh spinach
- ➤ 1 tablespoon MCT oil
- ➤ 1 teaspoon organic vanilla extract
- ➤ 6–8 drops liquid stevia
- ➤ 1½ cups unsweetened almond milk
- ➤ ½ cup ice cubes

How to Prepare

1. In a blender, put all the listed ingredients and pulse until creamy.

2. Pour the smoothie into two glasses and serve immediately.

Preparation time: 10 minutes
Total time: 10 minutes
Servings: 2

Nutritional Values

➢ *Calories 180*
➢ *Net Carbs 0 g*
➢ *Total Fat 18 g*
➢ *Saturated Fat 9 g*
➢ *Cholesterol 0 mg*
➢ *Sodium 161 mg*
➢ *Total Carbs 6.5 g*
➢ *Fiber 4.3 g*
➢ *Sugar 0.6 g*
➢ *Protein 2.4 g*

Matcha Smoothie

Ingredients

- ➢ 2 tablespoons chia seeds
- ➢ 2 teaspoons matcha green tea powder
- ➢ ½ teaspoon fresh lemon juice
- ➢ ½ teaspoon xanthan gum
- ➢ 10 drops liquid stevia
- ➢ 4 tablespoons plain Greek yogurt
- ➢ 1½ cups unsweetened almond milk
- ➢ ¼ cup ice cubes

How to Prepare

1. In a blender, put all the listed ingredients and pulse until creamy.
2. Pour the smoothie into two glasses and serve immediately.

Preparation time: 10 minutes
Total time: 10 minutes
Servings: 2

Nutritional Values

➢ *Calories 85*
➢ *Net Carbs 3.5 g*
➢ *Total Fat 5.5 g*
➢ *Saturated Fat 0.8 g*
➢ *Cholesterol 2 mg*
➢ *Sodium 174 mg*
➢ *Total Carbs 7.6 g*
➢ *Fiber 4.1 g*
➢ *Sugar 2.2 g*
➢ *Protein 4 g*

Creamy Spinach Smoothie

Ingredients

- ➢ 2 cups fresh baby spinach
- ➢ 1 tablespoon almond butter
- ➢ 1 tablespoon chia seeds
- ➢ 1/8 teaspoon ground cinnamon
- ➢ Pinch of ground cloves
- ➢ ½ cup heavy cream
- ➢ 1 cup unsweetened almond milk
- ➢ ½ cup ice cubes

How to Prepare

1. In a blender, put all the listed ingredients and pulse until creamy.

2. Pour the smoothie into two glasses and serve immediately.

Preparation time: 10 minutes

Total time: 10 minutes

Servings: 2

Nutritional Values

- ➢ *Calories 195*
- ➢ *Net Carbs 2.8 g*
- ➢ *Total Fat 18.8 g*
- ➢ *Saturated Fat 7.5 g*
- ➢ *Cholesterol 41 mg*
- ➢ *Sodium 126 mg*
- ➢ *Total Carbs 6.1 g*
- ➢ *Fiber 3.3 g*
- ➢ *Sugar 0.5 g*
- ➢ *Protein 4.5 g*

DESSERT RECIPES

Mocha Ice Cream

Ingredients

- ➤ 1 cup unsweetened coconut milk
- ➤ ¼ cup heavy cream
- ➤ 2 tablespoons granulated erythritol
- ➤ 15 drops liquid stevia
- ➤ 2 tablespoons cacao powder
- ➤ 1 tablespoon instant coffee
- ➤ ¼ teaspoon xanthan gum

How to Prepare

1. In a container, add all the ingredients (except xanthan gum) and with an immersion blender, blend until well combined.
2. Slowly, add the xanthan gum and blend until a slightly thicker mixture is formed.
3. Transfer the mixture into ice cream maker and process according to manufacturer's instructions.
4. Now, transfer the ice cream into an airtight container and freeze for at least 4–5 hours before serving.

Preparation time: 15 minutes
Total time: 15 minutes
Servings: 2

Nutritional Values

- *Calories 246*
- *Net Carbs 4.2 g*
- *Total Fat 23.1 g*
- *Saturated Fat 19.1 g*
- *Cholesterol 21 mg*
- *Sodium 52 mg*
- *Total Carbs 6.2 g*
- *Fiber 2 g*
- *Sugar 3 g*
- *Protein 2.8 g*

Raspberry Mousse

Ingredients

- ➢ 2½ cups fresh raspberries
- ➢ 1/3 cups granulated erythritol
- ➢ 1/3 cup unsweetened almond milk
- ➢ 1 tablespoon fresh lemon juice
- ➢ 1 teaspoon liquid stevia
- ➢ ¼ teaspoon salt

How to Prepare

1. In a food processor, add all the listed ingredients and pulse until smooth.

2. Transfer the mixture into serving glasses and refrigerate to chill before serving.

Preparation time: 10 minutes
Total time: 10 minutes
Servings: 4

Nutritional Values

- ➢ *Calories 44*
- ➢ *Net Carbs 4.3 g*
- ➢ *Total Fat 0.8 g*
- ➢ *Saturated Fat 0.1 g*
- ➢ *Cholesterol 0 mg*
- ➢ *Sodium 164 mg*
- ➢ *Total Carbs 9.4 g*
- ➢ *Fiber 5.1 g*
- ➢ *Sugar 3.5 g*
- ➢ *Protein 1 g*

Vanilla Crème Brûlée

Ingredients

- ➢ 2 cups heavy cream
- ➢ 1 vanilla bean, halved with seeds scraped out
- ➢ 4 organic egg yolks
- ➢ 1/3 teaspoon stevia powder
- ➢ 1 teaspoon organic vanilla extract
- ➢ Pinch of salt
- ➢ 4 tablespoon granulated erythritol

How to Prepare:

1. Preheat your oven to 350°F.

2. In a pan, add heavy cream over medium heat and cook until heated.

3. Stir in the vanilla bean seeds and bring to a gentle boil.

4. Reduce the heat to very low and cook, covered for about 20 minutes.

5. Meanwhile, in a bowl, add the remaining ingredients (except erythritol) and beat until thick and pale mixture forms.

6. Remove the heavy cream from heat and through a fine-mesh strainer, strain into a heat-proof bowl.

7. Slowly, add the cream in egg yolk mixture beating continuously until well combined.

8. Divide the mixture into 4 ramekins evenly.

9. Arrange the ramekins into a large baking dish.

10. In the baking dish, add hot water about half way of the ramekins.

11. Bake for about 30–35 minutes.

12. Remove pan from the oven and let it cool slightly.

13. Refrigerate the ramekins for at least 4 hours.

14. Just before serving, sprinkle the ramekins with erythritol evenly.

15. Holding a kitchen torch about 4–5-inches from top, caramelize the erythritol for about 2 minutes.

16. Set aside for 5 minutes before serving.

Preparation time: 20 minutes

Cooking time: 1 hour

Total time: 1 hour 20 minutes

Servings: 4

Nutritional Values

- ➢ *Calories 264*
- ➢ *Net Carbs 2.4 g*
- ➢ *Total Fat 26.7 g*
- ➢ *Saturated Fat 19.4 g*
- ➢ *Cholesterol 292 mg*
- ➢ *Sodium 31 mg*
- ➢ *Total Carbs 2.4 g*
- ➢ *Fiber 0 g*
- ➢ *Sugar 0.3 g*
- ➢ *Protein 3.9 g*

Lemon Soufflé

Ingredients

- ➤ 2 large organic eggs (whites and yolks separated)
- ➤ ¼ cups granulated erythritol, divided
- ➤ 1 cup ricotta cheese
- ➤ 1 tablespoon fresh lemon juice
- ➤ 2 teaspoons lemon zest, grated
- ➤ 1 teaspoon poppy seeds
- ➤ 1 teaspoon organic vanilla extract

How to Prepare

1. Preheat your oven to 375°F.

2. Grease 4 ramekins.

3. In a clean glass bowl, add egg whites and beat until foamy.

4. Add 2 tablespoons of erythritol and beat until stiff peaks form.

5. In another bowl, add ricotta cheese, egg yolks and remaining erythritol, and beat until well combined.

6. Now, place the lemon juice and lemon zest and mix well.

7. Add the poppy seeds and vanilla extract and mix until well combined.

8. Add the whipped egg whites into the ricotta mixture and gently, stir to combine.

9. Place the mixture into prepared ramekins evenly.

10. Bake for about 20 minutes.

11. Remove from oven and serve immediately.

Preparation time: 15 minutes

Cooking time: 20 minutes

Total time: 35 minutes

Servings: 4

Nutritional Values

- ➤ Calories 130
- ➤ Net Carbs 3.8 g
- ➤ Total Fat 7.7 g
- ➤ Saturated Fat 3.9 g
- ➤ Cholesterol 112 mg
- ➤ Sodium 114 mg
- ➤ Total Carbs 4 g
- ➤ Fiber 0.2 g
- ➤ Sugar 0.8 g
- ➤ Protein 10.4 g

Cottage Cheese Pudding

Ingredients

Pudding

- ➢ 1 cup cottage cheese
- ➢ ¾ cup heavy cream
- ➢ 3 organic eggs
- ➢ ¾ cup water
- ➢ ½ cups granulated erythritol
- ➢ 1 teaspoon organic vanilla extract

Topping

- 1/3 cup heavy whipping cream
- 1/3 cup fresh raspberries

How to Prepare

1. Preheat your oven to 350°F.

2. Grease 6 (6-ounce) ramekins.

3. In a blender, add all the ingredients (except cinnamon) and pulse until smooth.

4. Transfer the mixture into prepared ramekins evenly.

5. Now, place ramekins in a large baking dish.

6. Add hot water in the baking dish, about 1-inch up sides of the ramekins.

7. Bake for about 35 minutes.

8. Serve warm with the topping o heavy whipping cream and raspberries.

Preparation time: 10 minutes

Cooking time: 35 minutes

Total time: 45 minutes

Servings: 6

Nutritional Values

- Calories 226
- Net Carbs 3.3 g
- Total Fat 19.6 g
- Saturated Fat 11.5 g
- Cholesterol 147 mg
- Sodium 202 mg
- Total Carbs 3.7 g
- Fiber 0.4 g
- Sugar 0.7 g
- Protein 9 g

Egg Custard

Ingredients

- ➤ 5 organic eggs
- ➤ Salt, as required
- ➤ ½ cup Yacon syrup
- ➤ 20 ounces unsweetened almond milk
- ➤ ¼ teaspoon ground ginger
- ➤ ¼ teaspoon ground cinnamon
- ➤ ¼ teaspoon ground nutmeg
- ➤ ¼ teaspoon ground cardamom
- ➤ 1/8 teaspoon ground cloves
- ➤ 1/8 teaspoon ground allspice

How to Prepare

1. Preheat your oven to 325°F.
2. Grease 8 small ramekins.
3. In a bowl, add the eggs and salt and beat well.
4. Arrange a sieve over a medium bowl.
5. Through a sieve, strain the egg mixture into a bowl.
6. Add the Yacon syrup in eggs and stir to combine.
7. Add the almond milk and spices and beat until well combined.
8. Transfer the mixture into prepared ramekins.
9. Now, place ramekins in a large baking dish.
10. Add hot water in the baking dish about 2-inch high around the ramekins.
11. Place the baking dish in oven and bake for about 30–40 minutes or until a toothpick inserted in the center comes out clean.
12. Remove ramekins from the oven and set aside to cool.
13. Refrigerate to chill before serving.

Preparation time: 15 minutes
Cooking time: 40 minutes
Total time: 55 minutes
Servings: 8

Nutritional Values

- Calories 77
- Net Carbs 6 g
- Total Fat 3.8 g
- Saturated Fat 1 g
- Cholesterol 102 mg
- Sodium 116 mg
- Total Carbs 6.5 g
- Fiber 0.5 g
- Sugar 3.7 g
- Protein 3.8 g

Cream Cake

Ingredients

- ➢ 2 cups almond flour
- ➢ 2 teaspoons organic baking powder
- ➢ ½ cup butter, chopped
- ➢ 2 ounces cream cheese, softened
- ➢ 1 cup sour cream
- ➢ 1 cups granulated erythritol
- ➢ 1 teaspoon organic vanilla extract
- ➢ 4 large organic eggs
- ➢ 1 tablespoon powdered erythritol

How to Prepare

1. Preheat your oven to 350°F.

2. Generously, grease a 9-inch Bundt pan.

3. In a large bowl, add almond flour and baking powder and mix well. Set aside.

4. In a microwave-safe bowl, add butter and cream cheese and microwave for about 30 seconds.

5. Remove from microwave and stir well.

6. Add sour cream, erythritol and vanilla extract and mix until well combined.

7. Add the cream mixture into the bowl of flour mixture and mix until well combined.

8. Add eggs and mix until well combined.

9. Transfer the mixture into the prepared pan evenly.

10. Bake for about 50 minutes or until a toothpick inserted in the center comes out clean.

11. Remove from oven and put onto a wire rack to cool for about 10 minutes.

12. Carefully, invert the cake onto a wire rack to cool completely.

13. Just before serving, dust the cake with powdered erythritol.

14. Cut into 12 equal-sized slices and serve.

Preparation time: 15 minutes

Cooking time: 50 minutes

Total time: 1 hour 5 minutes

Servings: 12

Nutritional Values

- ➤ *Calories 258*
- ➤ *Net Carbs 3.5 g*
- ➤ *Total Fat 24.3 g*
- ➤ *Saturated Fat 9.6 g*
- ➤ *Cholesterol 96 mg*
- ➤ *Sodium 103 mg*
- ➤ *Total Carbs 5.5 g*
- ➤ *Fiber 2 g*
- ➤ *Sugar 0.9 g*
- ➤ *Protein 7.2 g*

Cookie Dough Fat Bombs

Ingredients

- ½ cup butter, softened
- 1/3 cup powdered erythritol
- ½ teaspoon organic vanilla extract
- ½ teaspoon salt
- 2 cups almond flour
- 2/3 cup 70% dark chocolate chips

How to Prepare:

1. In a large bowl, place the butter and with a hand mixer, beat until light and fluffy.

2. Add erythritol, vanilla extract, and salt, and beat until well combined.

3. Slowly, add flour, beating continuously until well combined.
4. Gently, fold in chocolate chips.
5. With a plastic wrap, cover the bowl and refrigerate for about 15–20 minutes before serving.
6. Make small equal-sized balls from the mixture.
7. Arrange the balls onto parchment-lined baking sheets and place in the refrigerator for at least 1 hour or until set completely.

Preparation time: 15 minutes
Total time: 15 minutes
Servings: 30

Nutritional Values

- *Calories 106*
- *Net Carbs 1.5 g*
- *Total Fat 9.7 g*
- *Saturated Fat 4 g*
- *Cholesterol 8 mg*
- *Sodium 62 mg*
- *Total Carbs 3 g*
- *Fiber 1.5 g*
- *Sugar 0.3 g*
- *Protein 2.3 g*

CONDIMENTS, SAUCES, & SPREADS RECIPES

Curry Powder

Ingredients

- ¼ cup coriander seeds
- 2 tablespoons mustard seeds
- 2 tablespoons cumin seeds

- ➢ 2 tablespoons anise seeds
- ➢ 1 tablespoon whole allspice berries
- ➢ 1 tablespoon fenugreek seeds
- ➢ 5 tablespoons ground turmeric

How to Prepare

1. In a large nonstick frying pan, place all the spices except turmeric over medium heat and cook for about 9–10 minutes or until toasted completely, stirring continuously.
2. Remove the frying pan from heat and set aside to cool.
3. In a spice grinder, add the toasted spices and turmeric, and grind until a fine powder forms.
4. Transfer into an airtight jar to preserve.

Preparation time: 10 minutes

Cooking time: 10 minutes

Total time: 20 minutes

Servings: 20

Nutritional Values

- ➢ *Calories 18*

- Net Carbs 1.8 g

- Total Fat 0.8 g

- Saturated Fat 0.1 g

- Cholesterol 0 mg

- Sodium 3 mg

- Total Carbs 2.7 g

- Fiber 0.9 g

- Sugar 0.1 g

- Protein 0.8 g

Poultry Seasoning

Ingredients

- ➤ 2 teaspoons dried sage, crushed finely
- ➤ 1 teaspoon dried marjoram, crushed finely
- ➤ ¾ teaspoon dried rosemary, crushed finely
- ➤ 1½ teaspoons dried thyme, crushed finely
- ➤ ½ teaspoon ground nutmeg
- ➤ ½ teaspoon ground black pepper

How to Prepare

1. Add all the ingredients in a bowl and stir to combine.
2. Transfer into an airtight jar to preserve.

Preparation time: 5 minutes

Total time: 5 minutes

Servings: 10

Nutritional Values

- ➤ *Calories 2*
- ➤ *Net Carbs 0.2 g*
- ➤ *Total Fat 0.1g*
- ➤ *Saturated Fat 0.1 g*
- ➤ *Cholesterol 0 mg*
- ➤ *Sodium 0 mg*
- ➤ *Total Carbs 0.4 g*
- ➤ *Fiber 0.2 g*
- ➤ *Sugar 0 g*
- ➤ *Protein 0.1 g*

BBQ Sauce

Ingredients

- ➤ 2½ (6-ounces) cans sugar-free tomato paste
- ➤ ½ cup organic apple cider vinegar
- ➤ 1/3 cup powdered erythritol
- ➤ 2 tablespoons Worcestershire sauce
- ➤ 1 tablespoon liquid smoke
- ➤ 2 teaspoons smoked paprika
- ➤ 1 teaspoon garlic powder
- ➤ ½ teaspoon onion powder
- ➤ Salt, as required
- ➤ ¼ teaspoon red chili powder

- ➤ ¼ teaspoon cayenne pepper
- ➤ 1½ cups water

How to Prepare

1. Add all the ingredients (except the water) in a pan and beat until well combined.
2. Add 1 cup of water and beat until combined.
3. Add the remaining water and beat until well combined.
4. Place the pan over medium-high heat and bring to a gentle boil.
5. Adjust the heat to medium-low and simmer, uncovered for about 20 minutes, stirring frequently.
6. Remove the pan of sauce from the heat and set aside to cool slightly before serving.
7. You can preserve this sauce in refrigerator by placing it into an airtight container.

Preparation time: 15 minutes
Cooking time: 20 minutes
Total time: 35 minutes
Servings: 20

Nutritional Values

- ➢ Calories 22
- ➢ Net Carbs 3.7 g
- ➢ Total Fat 0.1 g
- ➢ Saturated Fat 0 g
- ➢ Cholesterol 0 mg
- ➢ Sodium 46 mg
- ➢ Total Carbs 4.7 g
- ➢ Fiber 1 g
- ➢ Sugar 3 g
- ➢ Protein 1 g

Ketchup

Ingredients

- ➢ 6 ounces sugar-free tomato paste
- ➢ 1 cup water
- ➢ ¼ cup powdered erythritol
- ➢ 3 tablespoons balsamic vinegar
- ➢ ½ teaspoon garlic powder
- ➢ ½ teaspoon onion powder
- ➢ ¼ teaspoon paprika
- ➢ 1/8 teaspoon ground cloves
- ➢ 1/8 teaspoon mustard powder
- ➢ Salt, as required

How to Prepare

1. Add all ingredients in a small pan and beat until smooth.

2. Now, place the pan over medium heat and bring to a gentle simmer, stirring continuously.

3. Adjust the heat to low and simmer, covered for about 30 minutes or until desired thickness, stirring occasionally.

4. Remove the pan from heat and with an immersion blender, blend until smooth.

5. Now, set aside to cool completely before serving.

6. You can preserve this ketchup in the refrigerator by placing in an airtight container.

Preparation time: 10 minutes

Cooking time: 30 minutes

Total time: 40 minutes

Servings: 12

Nutritional Values

> *Calories 13*
> *Net Carbs 2.3 g*
> *Total Fat 0.1 g*

- ➢ Saturated Fat 0 g
- ➢ Cholesterol 0 mg
- ➢ Sodium 26 mg
- ➢ Total Carbs 2.9 g
- ➢ Fiber 0.6 g
- ➢ Sugar 1.8 g
- ➢ Protein 0.7 g

Cranberry Sauce

Ingredients

- ➤ 12 ounces fresh cranberries
- ➤ 1 cup powdered erythritol
- ➤ ¾ cup water
- ➤ 1 teaspoon fresh lemon zest, grated
- ➤ ½ teaspoon organic vanilla extract

How to Prepare

1. Place the cranberries, water, erythritol, and lemon zest in a medium pan and mix well.
2. Place the pan over medium heat and bring to a boil.

3. Adjust the heat to low and simmer for about 12–15 minutes, stirring frequently.
4. Remove the pan from heat and mix in the vanilla extract.
5. Set aside at room temperature to cool completely.
6. Transfer the sauce into a bowl and refrigerate to chill before serving.

Preparation time: 10 minutes
Cooking time: 15 minutes
Total time: 25 minutes
Servings: 6

Nutritional Values

- ➢ *Calories 32*
- ➢ *Net Carbs 3.2 g*
- ➢ *Total Fat 0 g*
- ➢ *Saturated Fat 0 g*
- ➢ *Cholesterol 0 mg*
- ➢ *Sodium 1 mg*
- ➢ *Total Carbs 5.3 g*
- ➢ *Fiber 2.1 g*
- ➢ *Sugar 2.1 g*
- ➢ *Protein 0 g*

Yogurt Tzatziki

Ingredients

- ➤ 1 large English cucumber, peeled and grated
- ➤ Salt, as required
- ➤ 2 cups plain Greek yogurt
- ➤ 1 tablespoon fresh lemon juice
- ➤ 4 garlic cloves, minced
- ➤ 1 tablespoon fresh mint leaves, chopped
- ➤ 2 tablespoons fresh dill, chopped
- ➤ Pinch of cayenne pepper
- ➤ Ground black pepper, as required

255

How to Prepare

1. Arrange a colander in the sink.

2. Place the cucumber into the colander and sprinkle with salt.

3. Let it drain for about 10–15 minutes.

4. With your hands, squeeze the cucumber well.

5. Place the cucumber and remaining ingredients in a large bowl and stir to combine.

6. Cover the bowl and place in refrigerator to chill for at least 4–8 hours before serving.

Preparation time: 10 minutes

Total time: 10 minutes

Servings: 12

Nutritional Values

➢ *Calories 36*

➢ *Net Carbs 4.2 g*

➢ *Total Fat 0.6 g*

➢ *Saturated Fat 0.4 g*

➢ *Cholesterol 2 mg*

➢ *Sodium 42 mg*

➢ *Total Carbs 4.5 g*

➢ *Fiber 0.3 g*

➢ *Sugar 3.3 g*

➢ *Protein 2.7 g*

Basil Pesto

Ingredients

- ➤ 2 cups fresh basil
- ➤ 4 garlic cloves, peeled
- ➤ 2/3 cup Parmesan cheese, grated
- ➤ 1/3 cup pine nuts
- ➤ ½ cup olive oil
- ➤ Salt and ground black pepper, as required

How to Prepare

1. Place the basil, garlic, Parmesan cheese, and pine nuts in a food processor, and pulse until a chunky mixture is formed.

2. While the motor is running gradually, add the oil and pulse until smooth.

3. Now, add the salt and black pepper, and pulse until well combined.

4. Serve immediately.

Preparation time: 10 minutes

Total time: 10 minutes

Servings: 6

Nutritional Values

> *Calories 232*
> *Net Carbs 1.4 g*
> *Total Fat 24.2 g*
> *Saturated Fat 3.8 g*
> *Cholesterol 7 mg*
> *Sodium 104 mg*
> *Total Carbs 1.9 g*
> *Fiber 0.5 g*
> *Sugar 0.3 g*
> *Protein 5 g*

Almond Butter

Ingredients

- 2¼ cups raw almonds
- 1 tablespoon coconut oil
- ¾ teaspoon salt
- 4–6 drops liquid stevia
- ½ teaspoon ground cinnamon

How to Prepare

1. Preheat your oven to 325°F.

2. Arrange the almonds onto a rimmed baking sheet in an even layer.

3. Bake for about 12–15 minutes.

4. Remove the almonds from oven and let them cool completely.

5. In a food processor, fitted with metal blade, place the almonds and pulse until a fine meal forms.

6. Add the coconut oil and salt, and pulse for about 6–9 minutes.

7. Add the stevia and cinnamon, and pulse for about 1–2 minutes.

8. You can preserve this almond butter in refrigerator by placing it into an airtight container.

Preparation time: 10 minutes
Cooking time: 15 minutes
Total time: 25 minutes
Servings: 8

Nutritional Values

➢ *Calories 170*
➢ *Net Carbs 2.4 g*
➢ *Total Fat 15.1 g*
➢ *Saturated Fat 2.5 g*
➢ *Cholesterol 0 mg*
➢ *Sodium 217 mg*
➢ *Total Carbs 5.8 g*
➢ *Fiber 3.4 g*
➢ *Sugar 1.1 g*
➢ *Protein 5.7 g*

Lemon Curd Spread

Ingredients

- ➢ 3 large organic eggs
- ➢ ½ cup powdered erythritol
- ➢ ¼ cup fresh lemon juice
- ➢ 2 teaspoons lemon zest, grated
- ➢ 4 tablespoons butter, cut into 3 pieces

How to Prepare

1. In a glass bowl, place the eggs, erythritol, lemon juice, and lemon zest.

2. Arrange the glass bowl over a pan of barely simmering water and oak for about 10 minutes or until the mixture becomes thick, beating continuously.

3. Remove from heat and immediately, stir in the butter.

4. Set aside for about 2–3 minutes.

5. With a wire whisk, beat until smooth and creamy.

Preparation time: 10 minutes

Cooking time: 10 minutes

Total time: 20 minutes

Servings: 20

Nutritional Values

➢ *Calories 32*

➢ *Net Carbs 0 g*

➢ *Total Fat 3.1 g*

➢ *Saturated Fat 1.7 g*

➢ *Cholesterol 34 mg*

➢ *Sodium 27 mg*

➢ *Total Carbs 0.2 g*

➢ *Fiber 0 g*

➢ *Sugar 0.1 g*

➢ *Protein 1 g*

Tahini Spread

Ingredients

- ¼ cup tahini
- 2 garlic cloves, peeled
- 3 tablespoons olive oil
- 3 tablespoons water
- 1½ tablespoons fresh lemon juice
- ¼ teaspoon ground cumin
- Salt and ground black pepper, as required

How to Prepare

1. Place all of the ingredients in a high-speed blender and pulse until creamy.

2. Pour the smoothie into two glasses and serve immediately.

Preparation time: 10 minutes
Total time: 10 minutes
Servings: 4

Nutritional Values

- *Calories 183*
- *Net Carbs 2.4 g*
- *Total Fat 18.7 g*
- *Saturated Fat 2.7 g*
- *Cholesterol 0 mg*
- *Sodium 58 mg*
- *Total Carbs 3.9 g*
- *Fiber 1.5 g*
- *Sugar 0.2 g*
- *Protein 2.7 g*

CHAPTER 5: 21-Day Meal Plan

Day 1

Breakfast: Broccoli Muffins

Lunch: Tuna Burgers

Dinner: Turkey Chili

Day 2

Breakfast: Eggs in Avocado Cups

Lunch: Stuffed Bell Peppers

Dinner: Roasted Cornish Hen

Day 3

Breakfast: Bacon Omelet

Lunch: Scallops in Garlic Sauce

Dinner: Pork Taco Bake

Day 4

Breakfast: Cheese Crepes

Lunch: Lamb Meatballs

Dinner: Chicken Parmigiana

Day 5

Breakfast: Chicken & Asparagus Frittata

Lunch: Creamy Zucchini Noodles

Dinner: Pork Taco Bake

Day 6

Breakfast: Pumpkin Bread

Lunch: Beef Burgers

Dinner: Beef Curry

Day 7

Breakfast: Ricotta Pancakes

Lunch: Shrimp in Butter Sauce

Dinner: Turkey Meatloaf

Day 8

Breakfast: Green Veggies Quiche

Lunch: Lamb Meatballs

Dinner: Salmon with Dill

Day 9

Breakfast: Broccoli Muffins

Lunch: Spinach in Creamy Sauce

Dinner: Rosemary Beef Tenderloin

Day 10

Breakfast: Cheddar Scramble

Lunch: Tuna Burgers

Dinner: Sticky Pork Ribs

Day 11

Breakfast: Yogurt Waffles

Lunch: Spinach in Creamy Sauce

Dinner: Shepherd's Pie

Day 12

Breakfast: Chicken & Asparagus Frittata

Lunch: Creamy Zucchini Noodles

Dinner: Seafood Stew

Day 13

Breakfast: Bacon Omelet

Lunch: Broccoli with Bell Peppers

Dinner: Stuffed Pork Tenderloin

Day 14

Breakfast: Green Veggies Quiche

Lunch: Lamb Meatballs

Dinner: Roasted Turkey

Day 15

Breakfast: Pumpkin Bread

Lunch: Scallops in Garlic Sauce

Dinner: Garlicky Prime Rib Roast

Day 16

Breakfast: Ricotta Pancakes

Lunch: Stuffed Bell Peppers

Dinner: Grilled Whole Chicken

Day 17

Breakfast: Cheddar Scramble

Lunch: Beef Burgers

Dinner: Tuna Casserole

Day 18

Breakfast: Yogurt Waffles

Lunch: Shrimp in Butter Sauce

Dinner: Spinach Pie

Day 19

Breakfast: Eggs in Avocado Cups

Lunch: Broccoli with Bell Peppers

Dinner: Roasted Leg of Lamb

Day 20

Breakfast: Cheese Crepes

Lunch: Beef Burgers

Dinner: Grouper Curry

Day 21

Breakfast: Broccoli Muffins

Lunch: Spinach in Creamy Sauce

Dinner: Pork with Veggies

CHAPTER 6: Prohibited Products List

Sugars

White

Brown

Maple syrup

Agave

Honey, Molasses

Confectioner's sugar

Granulated sugar

Grains

Rice, brown and white

Wheat

Barley

Maze

Corn

Farro

Sorghum

Millet

Oats

Oatmeal

White flour

All-purpose flour

Rice flour

Cornmeal

Beans

Canned beans

Kidney beans

Cannellini beans

Navy beans

Lentils

Black-eyed peas

Chickpeas

Chickpea flour

Fruits

Apples

Bananas

Peaches

Pears

Watermelon

Melon

Oranges

Mandarin

Clementine

Mango

Pineapple

Guava

Jackfruit

Dragon fruit

Vegetables

Potatoes

Sweet potatoes

Butternut squash

Yams

Dairy

Cow milk

Goat milk

Miscellaneous

Cola drinks

Sweet chocolates

Condensed milk

Fruit jams

Fast food

Flour bread

Pizza dough

Packed pie crust

Bakery items

Candies

Confectioneries

CHAPTER 7: Keto Diet Shopping List for Seniors

Poultry, Meat, & Seafood

4 (1½-pound) Cornish game hens

1 (4-pound) grass-fed whole chicken

3 pounds grass-fed chicken breast

11 (6-ounces) grass-fed boneless skinless chicken breasts

3 pounds grass-fed boneless, skinless chicken breasts

4 (6-ounce) grass-fed boneless, skinless chicken breast halves

8 (6-ounce) grass-fed skinless chicken thighs

1 (9-pound) whole turkey

1 (7-pound) bone-in turkey breast

3 pounds lean ground turkey

2½ pounds grass-fed beef chuck roast

1 (3-pound) grass-fed center-cut beef tenderloin roast

1 (10-pound) grass-fed prime rib roast

2 (4-ounce) grass-fed beef tenderloin steaks

4 (6-ounces) grass-fed beef tenderloin filets

2 ½ pounds grass-fed ground beef

1 (5-pound) grass-fed bone-in leg of lamb, trimmed

2 (2½-pounds) grass-fed racks of lamb

1 pound grass-fed ground lamb

1 pound pork loin

1 pound pork tenderloin

4 pounds pork rib

4 pounds lean ground pork

16 bacon slices

1 jar liver pate

6 (6-ounce) skinless, boneless salmon fillets

1 pound smoked salmon

1½ pounds skinless grouper fillets

1 (15-ounce) can water-packed tuna

16 ounces canned tuna in olive oil

2 (1½-pound) wild-caught trout

5 pounds shrimp

1¼ pounds fresh scallops

¼ pound bay scallops

¼ pound fresh squid

¼ pound mussels

Vegetables

6 heads broccoli

2 (12-ounce) packages riced cauliflower

1 pumpkin

10 zucchinis

2 (10-ounce) packages frozen spinach

1 (16-ounce) bag frozen chopped spinach

10 bags fresh spinach

1 bag fresh arugula

2 bags fresh baby spinach

8 green bell pepper

5 red bell pepper

1 carrot

3 pounds asparagus

1 bag fresh white mushrooms

3 bags fresh button mushrooms

½ cup Kalamata olives

6 bags tomatoes

1 bag cherry tomatoes

5 large English cucumbers

12 yellow onions

11 celery stalks

5 heads garlic

3 knobs fresh ginger

15 lemons

5 limes

12 heads lettuce

1 fresh red chili

1 green chil

3 Serrano peppers

2 jalapeño peppers

7 bunches fresh parsley

6 bunches fresh dill

3 bunches fresh mint

1 bunch fresh chives

8 bunches fresh cilantro

20 bunches fresh basil

4 bunches fresh rosemary

2 bunches fresh thyme

2 bunches fresh oregano

2 bunches scallion

Fruit

2 avocados

1 bag fresh strawberries

1 bag frozen strawberries

4 bags fresh raspberries

1 bag fresh cranberries

Dairy Products

12 tubs butter

1 tub unsalted butter

6 tubs plain Greek yogurt

4 jars mayonnaise

1 tub sour cream

11 tubs heavy cream

4 tubs heavy whipping cream

8 packages cream cheese

7 packages Parmesan cheese

1 package Parmigiano Reggiano cheese

7 packages cheddar cheese

1 package sharp cheddar cheese

7 packages mozzarella cheese

2 packages Swiss cheese

1 package provolone cheese

2 packages ricotta cheese

1 package feta cheese

1 package cottage cheese

Seasonings & Spices

2 bottles salt

2 bottles ground black pepper

1 bottle pumpkin pie spice

1 bottle ground allspice

1 bottle ground cinnamon

1 bottle ground nutmeg

1 bottle ground cloves

1 bottle ground cardamom

1 bottle ground ginger

1 bottle cumin seeds

1 bottle coriander seeds

1 bottle mustard seed

1 bottle anise seeds

1 bottle whole allspice berries

1 bottle fenugreek seeds

1 bottle ground cumin

1 bottle ground coriander

1 bottle dehydrated onion flakes

1 bottle granulated garlic

1 bottle garlic powder

1 bottle onion powder

1 bottle ground turmeric

1 bottle curry powder

1 bottle garam masala

1 bottle paprika

1 bottle smoked paprika

1 bottle cayenne pepper

1 bottle red chili powder

1 bottle red pepper flakes

1 bottle chili flakes

1 bottle fennel seeds

1 bottle lemon pepper

1 bottle Italian seasoning

1 pack ranch seasoning mix

1 bottle poultry seasoning

1 bottle taco seasoning

1 bottle lemon-pepper seasoning

1 bottle dried parsley

1 bottle dried rosemary

1 bottle dried thyme

1 bottle dried basil1 bottle dried oregano

1 bottle dried sage

1 bottle dried marjoram

Extras

97 organic eggs

9 cans unsweetened almond milk

7 cans unsweetened coconut milk

1 jar Italian dressing

2 bottles olive oil

1 bottle coconut oil

1 bottle sesame oil

1 bottle MCT oil

1 bag almond flour

1 bag superfine blanched almond flour

1 bag coconut flour

1 bag arrowroot starch

1 bag xanthan gum

1 bottle organic baking powder

1 bottle baking soda

1 bag flaxseed meal

1 bag chia seeds

1 bag poppy seeds

1 bag almonds

1 bag raw almonds1 bag pine nuts

1 bag walnuts

1 bag 70% dark chocolate chips

1 bag unsweetened vanilla whey protein powder

1 bottle matcha green tea powder

1 bottle cacao powder

1 bottle instant espresso powder

1 bottle instant coffee

1 tub almond butter

1 jar tahini

1 jar Dijon mustard

1 jar mustard powder

1 bottle chili sauce

1 bottle low-sodium soy sauce

1 bottle red boat fish sauce

1 bottle Worcestershire sauce

1 bottle liquid smoke

1 bottle organic vanilla extract

1 bottle organic lemon extract

2 bottles granulated erythritol

2 bottles powdered erythritol

1 bottle liquid stevia

1 bottle powdered stevia

1 bottle Yukon syrup

1 bottle organic apple cider vinegar

1 bottle balsamic vinegar

5 cans sugar-free tomato paste

1 jar sugar-free BBQ sauce

1 jar sugar-free ketchup

1 jar sugar-free HP steak sauce

1 can chopped green chilies

1 vanilla bean

Conclusion

Intermittent fasting, together with the ketogenic diet, can solve almost all the health issues that women over 50 years of age face every day. If you want to regain high rates of metabolism and want to feel young again, then try the most suitable method of intermittent fasting and complement this fasting regime with a low-carb ketogenic diet. This fasting keto program is capable of controlling weight gain and preventing all the health disorders that occur with aging. Try the fat-rich low-carb ketogenic recipes shared in this cookbook and experience the change yourself! Changes that come with aging are natural, and there is no medicinal treatment to prevent the process; however, it can be slowed down only through a better diet and a healthy lifestyle. This ketogenic fasting approach provides a perfect plan to achieve such health goals.

Resources

https://www.ncbi.nlm.nih.gov/pmc/articles/PMC2716748/

https://www.ncbi.nlm.nih.gov/pubmed/23651522

https://www.health.com/nutrition/keto-diet-grocery-list

https://www.nutribullet.com/blog/7-ways-a-keto-diet-is-perfect-for-menopause/

https://www.pcosdietsupport.com/pcos-symptoms/intermittent-fasting-for-pcos/

https://www.whitelotusclinic.ca/blog/dr-kelly-nd/intermittent-fasting/

https://ketodietapp.com/Blog/lchf/ketogenic-diet-and-menopause

https://www.eatthis.com/body-changes-after-50/

https://www.researchgate.net/publication/317858823_Fasting_as_possible_complementary_approach_for_polycystic_ovary_syndrome_Hope_or_hype

https://www.researchgate.net/publication/337691456_Intermittent_fasting_for_the_prevention_of_cardiovascular_disease

https://www.researchgate.net/publication/318498553_Metabolic_Effects_of_Intermittent_Fasting

Made in the USA
Columbia, SC
11 October 2020

22624809R00154